A Widower's Parable

1.23.23
S.E.R.E
(Survive, Evade, Resist, Escape)

Mo Thompson

ISBN:979-8-89663-333-4

Dedication

In the Name of Allah, the Most Merciful, the Most Compassionate. Alhamdulillah, all praises belong to Almighty Allah, the Lord of the worlds. Prayers and peace be upon His servants and messengers.

With heartfelt appreciation, I would like to extend special thanks to my mother, Lorraine Thompson, for her unconditional love and support during my darkest days. Your unwavering encouragement is unmatched; you are one of my greatest blessings. My sincere gratitude also extends to my trailblazing grandmothers, Artie Mosley and Louise Thompson and grandfather Isiah Thompson Jr. on my father's side.

May they Rest in Power. These incredible souls taught me how to walk as an upright man along the turbulent paths of life while keeping my vices in check and my faith strong.

To the many mentors I've had the privilege of meeting across the globe during my early college years and 20 years of military service, you are always in my thoughts and prayers. Know that your guidance and hard-earned lessons never fell on deaf ears. Each of you played a pivotal role in shaping me into the man I am today.

To my wife—you were my best friend, my counsel, and my partner in life. We shared everything—our hopes, our dreams, our lives—and I will miss you forever. Most of all, I will miss our intimate conversations and our shared passion for discovering new destinations. It was your dream to travel the world. This book is a tribute to how you inspired me to always be great, no matter how lonely the path may be.

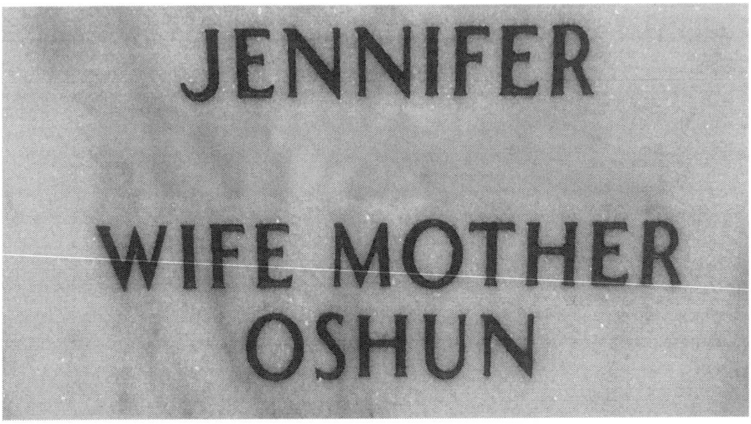

Acknowledgment

This book began as a therapeutic journal, inspired during one of my many "mental health" sessions with my therapist and through my daily meditation routine. With all the pain, love, promises, and fears I've endured, I am grateful for the resilience to face many challenges and periods of isolation, allowing me to stay focused on my purpose.

It was my willingness to sacrifice time away from activities and people that gave me the clarity to see that writing this book was my calling. I've planned for many things in my life, but authorship and being a widower are two roles I never expected to embrace.

My intention with this book is not to provide answers to life's questions but to spark the "freethinker" that resides within each of us. I hope my life story inspires you to hold fast to your dreams, even when life brings unexpected challenges and overwhelming heartbreak.

"Remember, God doesn't make mistakes."

Ghana Calls
by W.E.B. DuBois
STAFF ONLY

About the Author

Mo Thompson was born in Central Mississippi. His lifelong passion is to educate and provide resources for military transitions and career opportunities, as well as to offer a range of health and wellness services. He served 20 years in the U.S. Army, working in various fields, including Combat Engineering, Operations, Information Technology, and Human Resources. His military service included three tours in Iraq and Afghanistan and Civil Affairs projects in Latin America, Africa, and Italy, where he gained extensive experience in Civil Information Management, mental health, and self-care.

Mo holds a Master's degree in Information Systems from the University of North Texas and a Bachelor's degree in Business Management from the University of Tulsa, graduating with distinction in both programs.

Preface

I began writing this book exactly one year after my wife suddenly passed away, returning home from dinner. The guilt of Survivor's Remorse and the trauma of witnessing her soul transition left an indelible mark on my spirit—one that I know I may never fully remove. Yet, I have learned to harness that pain as a motivational tool. Writing was always my wife's passion, and now, this bittersweet endeavor—my first book—has emerged from the depths of my grief. I dedicate this book to my wife, Jennifer.

In the months following her passing, I struggled with Survivor's Remorse and PTSD, haunted by the feeling that I had failed to revive her long enough for the First Responders to arrive. While her death was profoundly heartbreaking, it served as a poignant reminder that "Life is for Living" and that tomorrow is never guaranteed. I realized that drowning in my grief and guilt was counterproductive.

About a week before our wedding anniversary, I made the conscious decision to share my story with the world after a break through therapy session. This book has unexpectedly become a true healing process and an additional layer of therapy. As I share my experiences, I confront past traumas, shortcomings, and reminders of my poor life choices. Yet, it has also become a beacon of courage, guiding me as I explore the parables of my life and navigate through the storms that have shaped me.

In this journey, I've embraced the principles of S.E.R.E.:

S—Survive your trauma and overcome it.

E—Evade the horrible circumstances and situations that seek to drag you down.

R—Resist the temptation to let those experiences affect your mood and keep negative people at bay.

E—Escape from societal norms and become a true "free thinker." At this stage, you can tap into the mystical powers of the Universe.

By embodying these principles, I am not just surviving; I am learning to thrive, and I hope my story inspires others to do the same.

Contents

Chapter 1: Grand Rising

The greeting "Grand Rising" emerged from spiritual and wellness circles as a more uplifting alternative to "good morning." It conveys a sense of optimism and positive energy, intended to create a hopeful outlook for the day ahead. It is more than just a unique way to say "Good morning." It is a phrase that carries deep significance, aiming to inspire a sense of spiritual and emotional awakening as you embark on a new day.

Unlike traditional greetings that acknowledge the time of day, "Grand Rising" conveys a more profound message. It signifies the opportunity for personal growth, new beginnings, and the cultivation of a positive mindset.

By greeting the day with "Grand Rising," you set a tone for a productive and fulfilling day ahead. It's a reminder to approach each day with intention, to stay present, and to make the most of the opportunities that come your way. This phrase encourages individuals to approach their day with mindfulness, recognizing that each morning is a chance to start afresh and to align their actions with their deeper values and aspirations.

By using this expression, individuals are reminded to appreciate the gift of a new day and to approach it with a hopeful and open heart. It serves as a gentle nudge to focus on life's positive aspects and see challenges as opportunities for growth rather than obstacles.

It aligns with the principles of self-awareness and self-empowerment, encouraging you to rise to your fullest potential. So, this phrase is more than a greeting; it's a call to action, motivating you to take charge of your day and to make choices that reflect your highest self.

The use of "Grand Rising" also connects individuals to a broader community of like-minded people who value personal growth and positivity. It creates a shared understanding and intention, reinforcing a collective commitment to living each day with purpose and awareness. This sense of connection and purpose starkly contrasts the environment I experienced in 1996 when I was 16 years old.

Attending school in rural Mississippi during that period felt like being trapped in a narrowly defined, tightly controlled environment. The small-town school system was characterized by its rigid structure and strong emphasis on conformity, which often felt suffocating.

The curriculum and daily routine were predictable and unchanging, creating a sense of monotony that I found particularly stifling. The limited scope of experiences offered by the school system was a stark contrast to what I yearned for. The school's small size meant fewer opportunities for diverse activities, extracurriculars, and intellectual exploration.

The social dynamics were similarly restrictive, with a close-knit community reinforcing a singular way of thinking and behaving. This lack of variety and the pressure to adhere to a specific set of norms left me feeling unfulfilled and restless.

I longed for an environment that was more dynamic and expansive—one that offered a broader range of experiences and allowed for personal growth and exploration. I yearned for educational and social opportunities that could challenge me and broaden my horizons, providing a richer, more stimulating experience.

The desire for something beyond the limitations of the rural school system was driven by a need for intellectual curiosity, personal development, and a sense of possibility that extended beyond the confines of the small-town setting.

While I was expected to engage with the academic material and show a genuine interest in my studies, I often felt like I was merely going through the motions. My real passions lay elsewhere, particularly in sports and social interactions.

At that stage, my primary focus was on sports and chasing after girls. I was deeply invested in the social dynamics of teenage life—trying to be a ladies' man to impress my friends and, more importantly, to connect with my father, who I admired greatly.

My father's approval was a significant motivator for me, and I often felt that my attempts to impress him and my friends were at odds with my school activities. This conflict created a sense of hypocrisy within me. I felt like I was living a dual existence: outwardly performing the role of a committed student while internally, I was more absorbed in my life's social and athletic aspects.

This internal struggle made me feel increasingly disconnected from the school environment, amplifying the sense that I was not being true to myself.

I found myself manipulating girls' emotions and feelings, reflecting on the behavior I had seen from my father more times than I cared to recall. Aside from getting into trouble, it seemed like the only way to capture his attention. Whether or not it was entirely accurate, it felt like this was the only path to engage with him.

The dissonance between my public persona and my private struggles was further exacerbated by the disturbing truths I witnessed within my own home. These revelations cast a long shadow over my understanding of morality and family.

From a young age, I saw my father engage in various acts of infidelity. These episodes typically occurred during times when my mother would insist on him taking me along on his outings or when I would plead persistently enough to accompany him.

These moments were unsettling and confusing, as they contradicted the moral and religious principles deeply ingrained in our family life. The disparity between the values preached, and the behavior witnessed left me grappling with a sense of disillusionment and questioning the authenticity of the beliefs that shaped our lives.

Despite being fully aware that I was exposing myself to situations I would rather have avoided, I was driven by a deep desire to spend time with my father. Our interactions were usually limited to fleeting moments or instances when my actions led to his disciplinary response, often involving his favored belt—a belt with a large, prominent buckle and a thick, formidable strap.

This belt became a symbol of the rare, direct engagements I had with him. Whenever I found myself in trouble, this very belt appeared, delivering the type of old-school punishment that was common in our household.

The discomfort and even fear associated with these moments starkly contrasted with my yearning for meaningful, positive time with him. The belt, a constant reminder of discipline and control, was far removed from the nurturing and supportive father figure I longed for. My efforts to be around him, even at the risk of witnessing things I would rather ignore, were fueled by a deeper need for connection and understanding with a father who was otherwise mostly distant and preoccupied.

Even now, years later, my father still doesn't truly understand who I am as his son. The disconnect between us persists, and despite my efforts to gain his attention through various means, I'm left with the lingering sense that he remains unaware of my true self.

Looking back, I recognize that I made a deliberate decision to distance myself from my father to safeguard my peace of mind. At the core of this decision was a deep-seated desire for a father figure who could offer me genuine guidance, support, and inspiration, someone I could turn to for advice and encouragement as I chased my dreams.

I longed for a paternal presence that would provide wisdom and motivate and uplift me through life's challenges.

In hindsight, my choice to address him by his first name rather than "Dad" might be more than just a casual preference. It could be a manifestation of this underlying emotional distance I have created. By opting for a more formal address, I may have subconsciously erected a barrier between us, an emotional shield to keep myself from fully investing in a father-child relationship.

This choice might reflect a deeper reluctance to open up and engage with him more personally and intimately. It's possible that by maintaining this distance, I have been trying to protect myself from potential disappointment or hurt while also shielding myself from the vulnerability of a closer relationship I had always craved but struggled to establish.

This pattern of emotional detachment, likely a defense mechanism, was deeply ingrained in my psyche. It was a survival tactic honed over years of navigating a complex and often contradictory family dynamic. The roots of this behavior, I believe, can be traced back to the broader cultural and generational context in which I was raised.

Both of my parents came from small, rural towns where the population was under 2,000 people. After finishing high school, they immediately entered the workforce and remained with their respective companies for over three decades. My father, in particular, dedicated an impressive 41 years to his employer.

The ethos of the era was one of quiet perseverance and spiritual devotion. Material possessions were seen as distractions from the ultimate goal of salvation.

A rigid adherence to religious doctrine and a strong work ethic were the cornerstones of a virtuous life. This worldview was deeply ingrained in the community, shaping everything from daily routines to aspirations.

The promise of a heavenly reward, far surpassing any earthly riches, served as a powerful motivator. This belief system created a society where contentment was cultivated over covetousness. People were encouraged to find fulfillment in their faith and their role within the community rather than seeking personal gain.

However, as I grew older, I began to question the underlying motivations driving these values. Was this simply a genuine expression of faith, or was it a more complex control system?

The stark emphasis on obedience, humility, and deferred gratification raised questions about the extent to which these beliefs were imposed rather than freely chosen.

The rigid structure of my parents' lives, defined by a relentless work ethic, unwavering religious observance, and a subdued public persona, created a sense of confinement. Their world seemed to revolve around a narrow set of expectations, leaving little room for individual expression or personal ambition.

This stark contrast between the professed values of faith and community and the lived experience of constraint and limitation created a dissonance within me. It forced me to examine how societal pressures and historical legacies might have shaped the beliefs and behaviors of those around me.

However, it wasn't until my twenties that the confines of my rural upbringing became painfully apparent. As I matured, it became clear that my ambitions and dreams extended far beyond the confines of rural Mississippi.

The quiet, predictable life of a small town felt increasingly limiting and stifling. I began to recognize that I was meant for something much larger and more dynamic than what my rural upbringing could offer.

In retrospect, I realized that my sense of boredom and disengagement had been a symptom of a deeper dissatisfaction. The routine of small-town life, with its narrow scope of opportunities and slower pace, left me feeling unfulfilled. I craved a sense of purpose and excitement that seemed unattainable within the confines of my surroundings.

The realization that I was meant for a life with broader horizons pushed me to seek out new experiences and challenges that would allow me to grow and pursue my aspirations more fully. This understanding marked a significant shift in my perspective, driving me to explore new possibilities and embrace a future that promised greater opportunities and personal growth.

For instance, I would often lose myself in daydreams of vibrant metropolises or the enchanting allure of Italy. The thought of immersing myself in the pulsating energy of a bustling city or exploring the rich tapestry of European history was intoxicating. I would visualize strolling down cobblestone streets, savoring authentic cuisine, and engaging with vastly different cultures. While my reality was confined to a small town, my imagination painted vivid pictures of a world beyond my reach.

My closest encounters with Europe were through the filtered lens of television and film, which offered romanticized glimpses into a life seemingly worlds away. These idealized portrayals fueled my longing for adventure and a taste of the unknown.

The surreal experience of actually living in Italy years later was a profound realization of the power of the human mind. It was as if a part of me had always known this was possible, subconsciously guiding my life's trajectory. This journey from childhood dreamer to European resident is evidence of the intricate interplay between imagination and reality. It's a reminder that our dreams, no matter how distant they may seem, hold the potential to become our reality.

This extraordinary experience has instilled in me a deep appreciation for the human capacity to envision a different life and to take steps, no matter how small, to make those visions tangible. It's a journey that inspires and shapes my perspective on life's endless possibilities.

Each morning, my wife and I greeted each other with "Grand Rising." It was more than a simple greeting—it was a celebration of our journey together. It symbolized our rise from a past full of limitations to a present brimming with possibilities. This daily exchange was a cherished reminder of how we transformed our lives, embracing each new day with hope and intention.

Chapter 2: Victory Lap

I fathered my children with two different women within a year, but unfortunately, I never built a strong relationship with either of them. Over time, I saw my children become pawns in a painful struggle. Rather than working toward a constructive co-parenting arrangement, the focus shifted to using my children as leverage—tools to extract more money from me or to settle personal grievances.

The real casualty in all of this was the time lost with my kids during their formative years. Their early childhood, a period that should have been filled with warmth and connection, was overshadowed by the conflict and manipulation that defined my interactions with their mothers. Every attempt I made to be present and involved was met with resistance, leaving me feeling more like an outsider than a parent.

The constant conflict and manipulation took a heavy toll on me, fueling deep anger and resentment toward both women. My journey toward finding peace began when I left Mississippi to attend college in Oklahoma.

It was a fresh start, an opportunity to distance myself from the turmoil of my past. To support my education and gain some financial stability, I joined the Army Reserves. This move helped cover my schooling expenses and gave me a sense of purpose and a way to regain control over my life. The structure and discipline of military service offered a new perspective and a chance to build a better future amidst the chaos I had left behind.

However, this new chapter came with its own set of formidable challenges. My time in the military, while providing valuable career opportunities and personal growth, felt like a double-edged sword—a "gift and a curse."

It meant leaving my children behind in Mississippi, a decision that carved out a deep and persistent emotional wound. The separation from them was not just a physical distance but an agonizing void that weighed heavily on my heart.

Every day apart felt like an eternity, amplifying the loneliness and heartache that haunted me. The distance was a constant source of pain, making the emotional burden of missing out on their early years even more acute. Adding to this heartache, I was reassigned overseas for two years as part of my service. This relocation took me further from the life I longed to be part of, intensifying my struggles. The miles between us seemed to stretch endlessly, deepening the chasm of separation and leaving me grappling with a profound sense of loss and isolation.

The distance separated us geographically and magnified the emotional gap, making every moment apart feel like a painful reminder of what I was missing. In the early 2000s, the technological limitations of the time made staying connected with my children and loved ones a difficult and frustrating experience. The absence of instant communication only heightened my sense of isolation. Being in a foreign country, grappling with a language barrier and cultural differences, compounded my feelings of alienation.

During this period, I wrestled with depression, struggling to cope with the emotional distance from my family and the overwhelming sense of disconnection. Yet, amidst the challenges, I started to learn how to manage my emotions more effectively. Through this process of self-discovery and emotional regulation, I began to find some peace. The discipline and structure of military life, combined with the necessity of navigating a new environment, eventually helped me build resilience and renewed hope for the future.

During my second year of college in Oklahoma, the weight of being a young father began to press down on me more heavily. Balancing the responsibilities of parenthood with the demands of school and military service was challenging. I was struggling to navigate my path in life, trying to reconcile my ambitions with my responsibilities as a father.

The pressures were intense, and finding a balance between my roles as a student, a soldier, and a dad was proving to be a difficult journey. I deeply yearned to be a true provider for both of my children and, more importantly, to be active in their lives. My goal was to offer them financial support and the emotional connection and involvement I felt I had missed growing up.

However, the strained relationships with their mothers only complicated this effort further, creating an even greater challenge in fostering a meaningful connection with my kids.

Reflecting on my upbringing, I realized how much I had missed out on. My father was more of an authoritarian figure, whose interactions were often characterized by a "do as I say" approach rather than the nurturing, mentoring, and guidance I longed for. This lack of bonding and connection in my childhood made me all the more determined to break that cycle and be different for my children.

In pursuit of this goal, I decided to leave college and give up my part-time job at UPS. It was a sacrifice, but I hoped it would pave the way for me to focus more on my role as a father and find a way to be there for my children more substantially and meaningfully.

I decided to commit to a full-time career in the military, envisioning it as a stable path that would provide for my family and give me the structure I needed. Over twenty years, I undertook three deployments and navigated through numerous relationships, many of which failed.

Looking back, I realize I often played a part in these failures through my self-sabotaging behaviors. It wasn't until I sought long-overdue therapy that I began to understand the root of my relationship patterns. In many ways, I had been replicating the same behaviors I witnessed growing up—patterns I had seen in my father's approach to his marriage and his extramarital affairs. I had become adept at operating in relationships in a way that mirrored his shortcomings, repeating the cycle of emotional detachment and dysfunction.

Through therapy, I came to the painful realization that my tendency to treat relationships as disposable, casual encounters stemmed from a deeper sense of incompleteness within myself. I was searching for something external to fill an internal void, never truly feeling whole or content with anyone. This insight was both eye-opening and challenging, exposing how my unresolved issues shaped my approach to love and connection.

In retrospect, I realized I had never truly understood what it meant to be fully devoted to a partner or to allow myself to be vulnerable in a relationship. My own experiences with intimacy were profoundly influenced by the toxic relationships that surrounded me growing up. I had no real model for healthy, committed relationships; instead, I was exposed to dysfunctional patterns that distorted my view of what a loving partnership should be.

The environment I grew up in was marked by the all-too-familiar scenario of a man having an affair outside his marriage while his wife either turned a blind eye or accepted the infidelity as part of their relationship dynamic. This toxic normalization of betrayal and emotional detachment shaped my understanding of relationships and intimacy.

I witnessed firsthand how such arrangements became the norm rather than the exception, creating a skewed perception of commitment and loyalty. Because of this, I struggled to grasp the concept of genuine devotion and vulnerability.

I didn't have a clear picture of what a healthy, supportive partnership looked like. Instead, my experiences were colored by a backdrop of acceptance of infidelity and emotional estrangement. This lack of positive examples made it difficult for me to cultivate and sustain meaningful connections, as I was operating from a place of confusion and misguided expectations.

A real relationship thrives on loyalty, where trust is steadfast and unwavering. It's rooted in truthfulness, ensuring that honesty guides every interaction. Communication is key, allowing for open dialogue and mutual understanding. Transparency keeps everything out in the open, preventing deceit and misunderstandings. It's not about glossing over flaws, ignoring betrayals, or pretending everything is fine when it's not. A genuine connection demands confronting issues head-on, facing imperfections with courage, and holding each other accountable with respect and integrity.

Navigating through multiple life challenges, especially those as intense as returning from deployment with severe PTSD, combat injuries, and the pressures of fatherhood, demands a delicate balance of self-care, support, and resilience. During such times, maintaining a level head involves acknowledging and validating your feelings while seeking professional help.

And so, after returning to Texas and seeking to re-establish a sense of stability, I chose to reconnect with my

Christian roots by renewing my faith and committing to regular church attendance.

Settling into Dallas, I found a church that felt like home—one where I could engage deeply with my beliefs and connect with a supportive community. Once I found that place, I joined the church choir, which provided me with a creative outlet and a sense of belonging and purpose.

Within this nurturing environment, I met a woman who, over time, became a significant part of my life. Our relationship blossomed, and I found myself envisioning a future together. When I proposed, it felt like a culmination of years of personal growth and self-discovery. I was truly convinced that I had reached a pivotal point of contentment and self-acceptance.

The journey through these experiences helped me feel comfortable and at peace with who I was, and I genuinely believed that I was in a wonderful place in my life, ready to embrace new beginnings and the promise of a shared future.

After re-establishing my Christian faith, settling into one city, and finding what I believed to be the love of my life, I felt a profound sense of accomplishment and contentment. I had worked through my past commitment issues and womanizing tendencies, and for the first time, I truly felt like I was on a stable, positive path.

My life seemed to fall into place in a way I had long hoped for—professionally, personally, and spiritually.

Despite this newfound sense of balance and happiness, the relationship faced an unexpected challenge. My partner's desire to have children eventually became a point of contention between us.

While I had been hopeful and committed to our future together, our differing visions for the future proved to be insurmountable. Just short of two years, our relationship ended, and it was a painful reminder that even when things seem perfect, not all outcomes align with our hopes.

To my surprise, she soon moved on, marrying later that same year and quickly embarking on the journey of parenthood.

In retrospect, I realize that I may have dodged a bullet. While our relationship had its issues, the fact that I didn't want any more children provided a way out, and it turned out to be a crucial factor in our separation. This experience taught me that sometimes what feels like a setback can be a blessing in disguise, as it opens the door to new opportunities and self-discovery.

However, looking back, I recognize that I could have approached the situation more maturely. In the aftermath of our breakup, while I wished her well and made an effort to check in occasionally, it became clear that my attempts at maintaining a positive connection were not always well-received.

Despite the end of our relationship, a part of my spirit continued to hold a place in my heart for her, reflecting the emotional complexity of moving on from someone you once deeply cared about.

The transition was challenging on multiple fronts. I left behind the comfort of suburban life—a symbol of stability and success—and moved to a weekly-rate hotel in the inner city. This shift represented more than just a physical relocation; it marked a profound search for peace of mind and a fresh start.

Many men in similar situations experience this same upheaval, finding themselves in less stable and more modest accommodations. This change often signifies a deeper quest for meaning and self-discovery.

This move was emblematic of a broader journey toward personal growth. It was a period marked by the need to reevaluate my life and priorities, seeking solace and clarity in new and often unexpected places. Despite the upheaval, it was a necessary step toward healing and understanding, revealing the resilience and adaptability required to navigate life's unpredictable challenges.

During this time, I began to explore and understand myself fundamentally. My modest living situation and the environment around me played a significant role in this self-discovery. Being in a weekly-rate hotel and witnessing the struggles of those living under similar circumstances exposed me to a stark reality I hadn't faced before.

Ironically, despite the challenges, this experience offered me a unique perspective on resilience and adaptability. For the first time in my life, I found myself technically homeless, moving from one weekly hotel to another over two months. Each place represented a temporary refuge, a place to rest and regroup while I navigated this tumultuous chapter.

Eventually, I secured an extended-stay hotel, which offered a more stable environment to call home temporarily. It was a modest and somewhat makeshift solution. Still, it provided the stability I needed while I sorted out the logistics of retrieving my personal belongings from the house I had just left. This period of transience and uncertainty forced me to confront aspects of my identity and priorities in ways I hadn't anticipated.

It became a profound journey of introspection, resilience, and growth, revealing the inner strength required to rebuild and move forward from life's unexpected challenges. I was determined to move forward with my life and retrieve my personal belongings without escalating into a domestic dispute. The goal was to handle the situation as amicably as possible, avoiding any unnecessary conflict.

As the months passed, spanning about six to seven months, I gradually began to experience a newfound level of inner peace. This period of tranquility was a stark contrast to the turbulence of the previous two years spent in our relationship.

During this period, the sense of peace I cultivated was profound. It felt like a restoration of balance and clarity that had been missing for a long time. I engaged in retrieving my belongings with a focus on resolution rather than contention.

Eventually, this led to a formal resolution through small claims court, where we both agreed to settle the matter legally. Although the court route was not ideal, it provided a clear path to finalize our separation and facilitated the recovery of my personal effects and some furniture.

The legal process, while impersonal, ultimately served as a practical solution to close that chapter and move forward with a renewed sense of peace and direction.

A few years later, I discovered a deep spiritual connection through Islamic teachings and devoted myself to practicing the Faith. This new path gave me a sense of spiritual fulfillment I had not experienced before. I realized that I had previously followed a faith presented to me as a child without any choice in the matter, as children have no say in the religion, names, or spiritual beliefs they inherit from their parents.

As I delved into my family's ancestry, tracing our roots back to West Africa, I uncovered that our lineage was part of the Yoruba tribe. This profound revelation sparked a renewed sense of connection to my heritage.

Inspired by this discovery, I began planning a pilgrimage to West Africa, eager to explore the land of my ancestors and immerse myself in the cultural and spiritual traditions of the Yoruba people. This journey was not just about spiritual exploration but also about reconnecting with a significant part of my heritage and understanding the deeper roots of my identity.

The Yoruba religion is one of the world's major spiritual traditions, with its roots deeply embedded in the cultural and historical fabric of West Africa, particularly in Southwestern Nigeria. It is a rich tapestry woven from a blend of indigenous tribal beliefs, myths, legends, proverbs, and songs.

Much like how Christians might reference the Psalms for spiritual reflection and guidance, the Yoruba religion draws on a vast array of oral traditions and spiritual practices to convey its teachings and values.

Yoruba spirituality is characterized by its diversity and adaptability, reflecting the complex interplay of various religious influences. It encompasses a broad spectrum of practices, including reverence for a pantheon of deities known as Orishas, each representing different aspects of life and nature. The Yoruba religion also integrates philosophical concepts, rituals, and ceremonies that are deeply connected to the rhythms of daily life and the natural world.

In contemporary practice, the Yoruba religion coexists with other faiths, such as Christianity and Islam, which many people in the Yoruba community follow alongside traditional beliefs. This pluralistic approach illustrates the religion's capacity to integrate and harmonize with other spiritual practices while preserving its own unique identity.

For individuals like myself, embracing Islam while honoring Yoruba traditions allows for a multifaceted spiritual journey that respects and celebrates both ancestral heritage and personal faith. The Yoruba religion's adaptability and inclusiveness reflect a broader cultural resilience and a deep-seated respect for diverse expressions of spirituality.

Many might question how blending different religious traditions is possible, but the process is quite straightforward once you understand the approach. The first step is to undergo a process of deprogramming from the beliefs and teachings instilled during your formative years. This means critically examining and reassessing the religious and spiritual doctrines you were taught as a child, allowing yourself the freedom to explore and understand them from a fresh perspective.

Approaching this exploration with an open mind is crucial. It involves setting aside preconceived notions and biases to engage with new ideas and practices genuinely. This open-mindedness creates space for integrating various spiritual traditions in a meaningful way.

When discussing this blending of faiths, I often advise people to undertake their own research. It's essential to dive into the sources, teachings, and practices of the traditions you are interested in rather than relying solely on inherited beliefs or the opinions of others.

Personal exploration and study enable you to develop your own understanding and come to original conclusions about what resonates with you. Recognizing that these conclusions may not always align with the dominant views within your social or religious circles is important.

Embracing a personal spiritual journey often means making unconventional or less popular choices among your peers.

However, this individuality in spiritual exploration can lead to a more authentic and fulfilling practice rooted in a deeper understanding of your heritage and personal beliefs. By balancing respect for traditional practices with a willingness to explore and adapt, you can create a harmonious and integrated spiritual path reflecting your ancestral roots and your current faith journey.

My first international trip with Jennifer was to Tulum. The Nipsey Hussle song, "Victory Lap," was filmed in the very place where we rented a yacht and celebrated—an experience that marked a personal victory amidst many challenges. That moment in Tulum symbolized more than just a getaway; it was a tangible reflection of overcoming struggles and savoring the victories along the way. Looking back, I realize that this journey has been filled with countless "victory laps," each one a testament to resilience, growth, and the ongoing quest for a better life.

Chapter 3: The Line Between Love and Hate

After my third deployment in 2011, I sought solace in my Christian faith. Finding a supportive community, I met a woman who seemed perfect. We became engaged, envisioning a future together. However, communication issues, trust problems, and a lack of support strained our relationship. Despite our initial excitement, our move together revealed hidden challenges. Within months, our dynamic shifted, leading to a difficult reality.

My fiancée, who had once felt like a best friend, began to focus on critiquing nearly every aspect of me. Our interactions, which had been filled with warmth and affection, started to be dominated by constant arguments and dissatisfaction.

During these frequent disputes, I found myself questioning her motives. I often said, "So, it seems like you don't actually like anything about me and were merely looking for a husband."

This sentiment reflected my growing frustration and confusion as I struggled to reconcile the idealized vision of our life together with the reality of the ongoing conflicts and criticisms. The gap between our expectations and day-to-day experiences widened, putting a strain on our relationship that neither of us had anticipated.

As our relationship progressed, my fiancée started to fixate on an idealized image of how we should present ourselves as a couple. Her preoccupation extended to every detail: how I dressed, how we should behave around friends, and how we should project our image to the outside world. This obsession with outward appearances and social expectations seemed to overshadow the genuine connection we had once shared.

The pressure to conform to this ideal was increasingly suffocating. Her rigid standards began to create a rift between us, making it difficult to enjoy simple moments together without the weight of constant scrutiny. It felt as though our relationship had shifted from a partnership built on mutual respect and love to a performance based on meeting external expectations.

It wasn't until a visit to her small rural hometown in Arkansas, where we went to announce our engagement to her family that I began to uncover the root of this obsession. During the visit, I witnessed firsthand the dynamics of her family life and how they influenced her views and behavior.

Her mother, who was in her third marriage, displayed a controlling and toxic demeanor that extended to every aspect of her relationships. She meticulously controlled her current husband's every move and seemed to impose similar expectations on those around her.

This experience shed light on the underlying issues driving my fiancée's behavior. It became clear that her mother's toxic relationship patterns and controlling tendencies had profoundly impacted her own outlook on relationships and expectations. The intense focus on appearances and adherence to a particular image were not just personal preferences but reflections of a broader pattern she had learned from her mother's example. Understanding this background helped me make sense of the challenges we faced, but it also highlighted the deeper issues we needed to address.

On the second day of our visit to her hometown, it became increasingly apparent that both my fiancée and her mother were deeply influenced by the narrow-minded traditions and routines prevalent in their rural Southern community.

Her mother's controlling behavior and obsessive focus on appearances and societal status were not just personal quirks but deeply rooted in the conservative, traditional beliefs that dominated their lives. It was clear that her mother had instilled in her a belief system that equated marital status and sexual activity with moral worth.

The notion that failing to secure a husband or engaging in sex outside of marriage would condemn someone to hell was a fear that had been ingrained in her from a young age. This perspective influenced her behavior and shaped her expectations for our relationship.

This revelation was a turning point for me. It illuminated why my fiancée was so fixated on our image and our adherence to traditional norms. It wasn't merely about personal preference but rather a reflection of the deep-seated values she had internalized from her upbringing.

Reflecting on this experience, I would advise anyone considering a serious commitment, like marriage, to understand their partner's background and influences thoroughly. Knowing someone's detailed history and the factors that have shaped their beliefs and behaviors can provide crucial insight into how they approach relationships.

This awareness can help assess compatibility and address potential issues before making a significant life decision. Exploring and understanding these aspects can prevent misunderstandings and ensure that both partners are on the same page about their values and expectations.

Whether we want to admit it or not, our upbringing and the environment in which we grow up profoundly impact the kind of adults we become.

For me, the breaking point in the relationship came when her controlling tendencies began to infiltrate the most personal aspect of our lives—our bedroom. When we began to have sex a year into our relationship, it became clear that it was on her terms alone. Her preferences scheduled and dictated every intimate moment, leaving little room for mutuality or spontaneity. This wasn't just about physical intimacy but about control—a deeper issue that started to affect our entire dynamic.

Over time, the reality of the situation began to sink in. I found myself consistently sidelining my own happiness to accommodate her rigid expectations. This pattern of self-sacrifice eventually wore me down.

As a result, I started to harbor growing resentment toward her. The constant pressure and lack of control over my own needs began to take its toll, leading me to self-sabotage the relationship in ways I wasn't always proud of. I grappled with a sense of guilt for misleading her. I knew that staying in the relationship under these toxic conditions was not fair to either of us, but I also understood that my actions were driven by a desperate need to escape a stifling environment.

The inner conflict of wanting to protect her feelings while struggling to protect my own well-being created a storm of emotions and moral dilemmas. Ultimately, I decided to heed the signs that seemed to guide me—a series of indicators from the Universe or a higher power suggesting it was time to move on. With about four months left before our wedding date, I made the difficult decision to end it.

Breaking up was not just an escape but a necessary step to reclaiming my own sense of self and well-being. It was a choice driven by the need to honor my own happiness and to recognize that the relationship had become untenable due to the toxic dynamics that had taken hold.

In the end, this experience served as a harsh but vital lesson in the importance of mutual respect and personal boundaries in any relationship. It was a journey that, while painful, paved the way for deeper self-understanding and the realization that true fulfillment comes from being in a partnership where both individuals' needs and happiness are valued equally.

About a year after the breakup, when I found out about my ex's pregnancy through her Facebook, I was shocked, to say the least. The woman I had once considered my soulmate was now married and expecting a child less than a year after our relationship ended. This unexpected turn of events intensified my struggles with what I now recognize as unresolved "Daddy Issues," a topic I have yet to address through therapy.

In the years that followed, I made a conscious decision to become emotionally unavailable. My rationale was straightforward: I wanted to focus on healing and becoming whole before introducing someone new into my life.

I felt it was essential to work through my own issues and find a sense of completeness within myself before I could genuinely engage in a healthy and fulfilling relationship with another person. This period of emotional withdrawal was a necessary step in my journey towards self-recovery and personal growth.

The five stages of rebound dating—Pre-Rebound, The Honeymoon Stage, The Reality and Conflicts Stage, The Nostalgia and Comparison Stage, and The Epiphany Stage—are often seen as a typical progression after a breakup. However, I was determined to sidestep these stages and avoid falling into the trap of rebound relationships.

Instead of diving into another relationship to fill the void left by my previous partner, I chose to invest in myself. I established a structured daily routine that included morning meditation, regular exercise, and dedicated time for reading.

I consciously reduced my television and social media consumption to create a more balanced and mindful lifestyle. This approach helped me focus on personal growth and self-improvement rather than seeking external validation or comfort.

By focusing on my own well-being, I aimed to avoid the pitfalls of rebound dynamics and the potential negative effects of energy transfer. My goal was to become self-sufficient and emotionally resilient, ensuring that any future relationship would be entered into from a place of strength and clarity rather than as a reaction to unresolved issues from the past.

Rebound relationships often stem from an urge to quickly fill the emotional gap left by a former partner. The impulse to engage with someone new can be strong, driven by the need to alleviate loneliness or distract from the pain of a breakup. In these relationships, the concept of "energy transfer" becomes significant.

When people are in close relationships, they naturally exchange energy, emotions, and even habits. This transfer can be intense and often unrecognized, blending emotional states that may not align with one's true feelings or needs.

Whether positive or negative, energy transfer in relationships significantly impacts all parties involved. The dynamics and status of the relationship at any given time can deeply influence the nature of this energy transfer.

Sexual interactions, in particular, can greatly amplify these emotional exchanges, intensifying both positive and negative energy between partners. When the energy transferred is positive, it can be profoundly uplifting and beneficial, fostering mutual growth and a deep sense of connection. Positive energy transfers can enhance the overall well-being of those involved, creating a nurturing and supportive environment where both partners thrive.

Conversely, when the energy being transferred is negative, it can lead to emotional turbulence and conflict. Negative energy transfers can exacerbate feelings of frustration, resentment, or sadness and may contribute to the deterioration of the relationship.

The phrase "A Thin Line Between Love and Hate" encapsulates this dynamic, highlighting how easily emotions can shift from deep affection to intense dislike if the energy exchanged is not managed responsibly. For individuals with a heightened sensitivity to emotional energy—such as empaths—the impact of these transfers can be even more pronounced.

As someone who identifies as an empath, you have a natural ability to perceive and absorb the emotions and energy of others. This sensitivity means you are more acutely aware of the emotional states around you and may find it challenging to separate your own feelings from those of your partner. You experience the emotional highs and lows of relationships more intensely. Positive energy can be deeply enriching, but negative energy can be overwhelming and draining.

As an empath, it's crucial to be mindful of how you engage with others and set boundaries that protect your emotional well-being. This involves being selective about who you allow into your life and how you manage the exchange of emotional energy.

By understanding and managing these dynamics, you can better navigate relationships, ensuring that you engage in fulfilling and healthy connections. This self-awareness helps maintain balance and protect your emotional health, allowing you to foster relationships that support and enhance your personal growth.

My empathic abilities, combined with my Cancerian personality traits, made me exceptionally sensitive to the emotions of others, especially those I was romantically involved with. This heightened emotional awareness allowed me to deeply connect with my partner's feelings and experiences, often intuitively understanding their needs and emotional states.

However, this intense emotional attunement also came with its challenges. The very qualities that allowed me to connect so deeply with others also made it difficult to establish and maintain clear boundaries between my own emotions and those of my partner. It was often hard to differentiate where my feelings ended and where theirs began.

This lack of clear emotional boundaries could lead to a sense of being overwhelmed or engulfed by the emotional dynamics of the relationship, making it challenging to maintain a balanced perspective.

Compounding this difficulty was an underlying trust issue—something I wouldn't fully recognize or address until years later. Trust issues often stem from past experiences and can affect how we interact with others. They can lead to apprehensions about vulnerability, fear of betrayal, or doubts about the reliability of others.

These trust issues created an additional layer of complexity in relationships. They made it harder to open up and rely on others fully, even when my empathic abilities might have otherwise guided me toward deeper connections.

In retrospect, these challenges were not just obstacles but also critical areas for personal growth. They highlighted the need for developing stronger boundaries and addressing unresolved trust issues. Understanding and working through these aspects became crucial for fostering healthier relationships and achieving emotional balance.

By recognizing the impact of my empathic abilities and trust issues, I could start to take steps toward improving how I interacted with others. This involved learning to set clearer emotional boundaries, developing strategies for managing my sensitivity, and seeking to resolve underlying trust issues.

These efforts were essential for creating a more harmonious and balanced approach to relationships, allowing me to build connections that were both emotionally fulfilling and grounded in trust and mutual respect.

When your mind is free from distractions and fully focused, you open yourself up to the potential to connect with the mystical forces of the Universe. This concept is often described as "Speaking it into Existence" or Manifestation. I prefer to call it "Tap in and Tune In."

Being tapped into the right state of mind allows you to mentally tune into the Universe's powerful energies. I firmly believe that with discipline and a focused mindset, you can influence the outcomes of your life. You can enter a "Zone" that facilitates extraordinary achievements by aligning yourself with the right frequency.

This alignment is similar to the inspirations behind Shakespeare's great works, the groundbreaking innovations of famous inventors, or Einstein's cosmic theories.

Throughout history, some of the most remarkable figures in literature, science, and innovation have achieved extraordinary feats of creativity and discovery. Think of Shakespeare's profound plays, the revolutionary inventions of Thomas Edison, or Einstein's groundbreaking theories of relativity. How did they tap into such brilliance? The answer lies in their ability to connect with a source of information that transcends ordinary reality.

These historic individuals seemed to have accessed deeper knowledge and insight, suggesting that their creative processes were influenced by a profound connection to the Universe's fundamental energies.

This connection isn't about witchcraft or blasphemy; rather, it's about accessing the mind's vast potential, tapping into areas that are typically beyond our everyday awareness.

Currently, we use only a fraction of our brain's potential in most of our daily activities. This limitation restricts our cognitive abilities and problem-solving skills. But what if we could learn to access and integrate multiple parts of our brain simultaneously rather than using them in isolation?

Envision upgrading your current capabilities from a standard laptop to a high-performance supercomputer. Such an enhancement would allow you to process information more efficiently and deeply. You could unlock new levels of creativity, understanding, and achievement by harnessing the full range of your cognitive resources.

Accessing the full potential of our brains could enable us to achieve extraordinary things. It would mean improving our problem-solving and creative capacities and better aligning with the Universe's energy. This expanded mental capacity could lead to breakthroughs in various fields, from scientific discoveries to artistic creations, making seemingly unattainable goals more accessible and manageable.

The key to this transformation lies in learning how to tap into and utilize these deeper levels of our consciousness.

Practices such as meditation, mindfulness, and focused discipline can help us unlock these potentials. By doing so, we align ourselves more closely with the universe's rhythms and gain access to a richer, more expansive understanding of reality.

Connecting with this broader source of knowledge and energy allows us to transcend ordinary limitations and achieve greater things, much like the historical figures who have inspired us with their genius.

"The Thin Line Between Love and Hate" was Jennifer and my favorite movie. Its insightful portrayal of how easily passion can turn into resentment resonates deeply with the experiences we've explored. The film's blend of drama and dark humor reflects the complex nature of relationships, reminding us of the fine line between love and conflict and the importance of understanding and managing those dynamics.

Chapter 4: Ascension (Don't Ever Wonder)

Ascension is the act of rising to a higher position or level of importance, success, or rank. In my case, it reflects my journey over two decades of traveling the world with the military, experiencing life from a unique perspective. This international exposure to diverse cultures and people illuminated my potential and reassured me that I wasn't just a strange outcast or a loner marching to my own beat.

As I navigated various countries and formed connections with individuals from all walks of life, I began to see the world through a different lens—one that celebrated individuality while also cherishing community.

During my travels, I encountered people whose values and aspirations mirrored my own, individuals who resonated with my way of thinking and encouraged me to embrace my true self. These interactions sparked a profound realization: the importance of surrounding myself with those who inspire and challenge me.

The old proverb "Birds of a feather flock together," became increasingly meaningful, as did my favorite saying, "Lions roam with other lions." Both emphasize the power of connection and the necessity of surrounding ourselves with like-minded individuals who propel us forward.

Lions symbolize courage, power, strength, and leadership—qualities I sought to embody in my own life.

Their fierce, tenacious spirit and inherent dominance reminded me that I have the capacity to lead and make an impact. As I adopted this mindset, I began to consciously curate my circle, seeking out those who shared my vision and ambitions. I realized that true loyalty should not be misplaced; it should be directed towards those who uplift and inspire us rather than those who anchor us to a past that no longer serves our growth.

With this shift in perspective, I sought environments that fostered growth and innovation. Whether through professional networking or engaging in activities aligned with my passions, I was drawn to communities that nurtured my aspirations.

I learned that ascension is not just a solitary journey but a collective one, where mutual support and shared experiences lead to greater heights. My travels became a means of exploration and a vital part of my self-discovery. I found wisdom in every corner of the globe. Each culture offered unique insights into leadership, resilience, and the human experience. I absorbed these lessons, transforming them into tools for my ascension.

In embracing the lion's mindset, I also recognized the importance of vulnerability and authenticity. True strength lies in dominance and the ability to connect deeply with others and lead with empathy. This balance of courage and compassion became the cornerstone of my leadership style, enabling me to forge meaningful relationships and inspire others to rise alongside me.

Ultimately, my journey is a testament to the transformative power of connection and the unwavering belief in my own potential. Each step I take toward ascension is grounded in knowing I am not alone. I walk alongside fellow lions, each determined to carve our paths while uplifting one another.

However, the more I distanced myself from home, my perspective evolved. I started to see the world from a vantage point that few do. Limitations that once held me back faded away; I no longer felt inadequate or undeserving of a fulfilling life. The burdens of guilt and survivor's remorse no longer haunted me.

Each new experience felt like adding a layer to a beautiful story, showing me colors and patterns I had never seen before. I found myself in busy cities, peaceful landscapes, and lively communities that welcomed me as if I belonged.

The stories of those around me—their dreams and struggles—helped me understand what it means to be human. I realized that my story, while unique, was part of a bigger story of strength and hope.

There were times when I felt guilty about leaving my home state and family behind, especially as my visits became less frequent. Each return felt like walking a tightrope; I struggled between my memories and the new life I was creating. I wanted to leave my past behind, worried that revisiting it would undo my progress. But I learned that my journey wasn’t just about putting distance between me and my past; it was about becoming who I was meant to be.

I discovered that my roots didn't have to cause conflict. Instead, they could be a strong base for my future. Talking with my family showed me that their struggles and victories were just as important, reminding me that distance didn't mean I had abandoned them. We shared laughs and tears, reconnecting despite the miles between us.

As I traveled further, I realized the importance of balance. I learned to carry my past with me, not as a weight, but as a source of strength. Each visit home became a chance to reconnect, to share my experiences, and to hear theirs. My upbringing became part of my present, enriching my understanding of both.

Through this journey, I also began redefining what "home" meant. It was less about a physical place and more about how I felt—like belonging, acceptance, and love. My heart grew to include the people I met, the lessons I learned, and the cultures I experienced. Every friendship and encounter added to my identity.

By embracing this journey, I found freedom. I was no longer held back by guilt or fear; instead, I was driven by a desire to live fully and authentically. I understood that my unique path was part of a shared quest for meaning and connection. With this realization, I stepped confidently into the future, ready to create my destiny while honoring the past that shaped me.

In Yoruba culture, "Igoke" embodies the concept of ascension, encompassing mental and spiritual elevation through a transformative journey involving shedding old habits and beliefs. This process can be personal or collective, often shared with a partner, close friend, or family member, fostering an environment of support and mutual growth.

Ascension, commonly associated with figures like Jesus, highlights the potential for profound transformation while still alive, emphasizing that it is not merely a physical departure but a deepening of consciousness.

Those attuned to this journey may experience themselves as multi-dimensional beings, accessing higher wisdom and emotions that enrich their own lives and positively impact those around them.

Ultimately, "Igoke" invites individuals to embrace this holistic growth, contributing to a collective upliftment that fosters deeper connections and elevated consciousness within their communities.

When my wife passed away, I experienced profound grief that often left me in tears at unexpected moments throughout the day. I found myself pleading with Allah to rise from bed simply. Even after several years, there are still days and moments when that sorrow feels overwhelming.

My wife and I used to explore topics like mental and spiritual ascension, the powers of the universe, and methods for cultivating a more focused and disciplined mind together. Our shared curiosity about unlocking the hidden potentials within our minds fueled many late-night discussions.

Humans are widely believed to utilize only about 10% of their brain capacity while awake. Advanced imaging techniques, such as MRI and PET scans, reveal that our brains engage in many activities simultaneously during sleep.

This underscores the importance of dreams; they serve as a mechanism for clearing out subconscious clutter, functioning much like a mental recycling bin. Just as a device with a full memory can experience glitches or malfunctions, our minds need this nightly reset to maintain clarity and function.

Therefore, prioritizing 7 to 9 hours of sleep each night is crucial for our physical and mental health. This rest helps restore energy, supports cognitive function, enhances mood, and strengthens the immune system, ensuring we can tackle each day with clarity and resilience. Prioritizing adequate sleep is an investment in our overall well-being.

This process helps us process emotions and experiences and allows us to tap into deeper layers of consciousness, making room for personal growth and understanding. The journey of healing and self-discovery is ongoing, and I continue to explore the vast potential that lies within, inspired by the discussions we shared.

Would you believe me if I said that we all possess the power to control our dreams and interpret them in ways that enrich our waking lives? This ability can be likened to having the "key to the city," as an old military phrase suggests. It begins with cultivating a clear and open mind, often involving stepping outside conventional thinking and ways of operating.

This non-traditional approach may raise eyebrows among family and friends who might not fully grasp the depths of your spiritual journey. They could perceive your exploration as a departure from your spiritual upbringing or religious beliefs, leading to misunderstandings.

However, it's crucial to remember that the path to spiritual awakening and self-discovery is uniquely personal. Not everyone will resonate with your experiences or the methods you choose to explore. This journey may require you to embrace practices like lucid dreaming, meditation, or even journaling about your dreams to gain deeper insights.

As you delve into these practices, you might find that they illuminate hidden aspects of your psyche, reveal truths about your emotional state, or guide you toward personal growth. It's natural to feel the weight of external opinions, but I advise tuning out the noise. Trust your intuition and stay committed to the path that feels right for you, even if it diverges from the expectations of those around you.

Spirituality is not a one-size-fits-all journey; it's an evolving process that requires courage, openness, and self-compassion. By nurturing your connection to your dreams and the wisdom they hold, you pave the way for profound transformation, allowing you to embrace your true potential while respecting your chosen path.

Every culture has its own meanings for the signs and symbols we see in our dreams. Yoruba culture has a rich tradition of interpreting these dream symbols, which have been understood over many years. These symbols are meant to help you understand your dreams' messages, not scare you. By recognizing these messages, you can take steps to make them a reality, essentially "speaking them into existence."

While no one can predict the future, our dreams often give us clues about what might happen. Paying attention to these clues is important so you can better navigate your life. For example, symbols like water can represent your emotions, and animals might show different parts of your personality. By interpreting these symbols, you can gain valuable insights that help you face challenges and seize opportunities.

Engaging with your dreams lets you take charge of your life. Each symbol has meaning and potential, guiding you through your current situation and helping you see possible future paths. By exploring what these symbols mean, you empower yourself to make informed choices, leading to personal growth and fulfillment. Ultimately, understanding your dreams helps you live more consciously and align your actions with your true self.

As I shared earlier, growing up in Mississippi, I was influenced by traditional Southern values, strict Baptist teachings, the challenges of poverty, and the ongoing effects of racism and segregation.

Even in the late 90s, many Black individuals in Mississippi struggled to claim their part of the American dream. It would have been simple to allow this environment to shape my identity and control my future. Instead, I chose to take action, rejecting a mindset of complaints and passivity.

This proactive approach became a central theme in the deep conversations my wife and I often engaged in about the significant choices that shape the "Matrix" we navigate daily. We recognized that many people live under various forms of control without even realizing it, influenced by societal norms, cultural expectations, and inherited beliefs.

This led us to ponder some thought-provoking questions: Have you ever truly examined why you hold the beliefs you do? For instance, would you still identify as Christian today if a different religion had been introduced to you during your formative years? Would your views on race remain the same? Would you still gravitate toward the same types of food and flavors?

These inquiries invite us to reflect on the myriad influences that mold our identities and beliefs, often without conscious awareness. Our upbringing, community, and cultural context play crucial roles in shaping how we see the world. They can dictate everything from our values and morals to our preferences and lifestyle choices. For instance, the traditions we inherit, the people we associate with, and even the media we consume contribute to a framework of understanding that can feel rigid and unchangeable.

By questioning these influences, we open ourselves to a deeper understanding of who we are and why we think the way we do. This process encourages us to explore alternative perspectives and challenge assumptions that may no longer serve us. It can be liberating to realize that our beliefs and preferences are not fixed but rather adaptable, shaped by experiences and choices.

Ultimately, these discussions helped us recognize the importance of critical thinking and self-reflection. They served as a reminder that we have the power to redefine our identities and beliefs, stepping outside the confines of our individual "Matrix."

"Ascension (Don't Ever Wonder)" by Maxwell holds a special place in my heart. I would sing it to Jennifer often, pouring my feelings into every note and lyric. The smooth melodies and soulful rhythm captured the essence of our connection. Each time I sang, I felt as though I was sharing a piece of my soul with her, expressing my hopes, dreams, and deep affection.

Chapter 5: Brown Sugar

During my time in isolation, I focused on clearing my mind and eliminating negative thoughts. I eliminated distractions and worked on being more disciplined. As I did this, I felt connected to a positive energy around me. This energy helped me take control of my life, and soon, everything went my way.

I was amazed at how quickly I regained what I had lost in the past year—three times more than I expected and in half the time. I also started achieving personal goals I had set for myself long ago. Each day, I felt more motivated and confident.

I made small changes to my daily routine, like journaling and meditating, which helped me stay grounded and focused. I noticed improvements in my health, my relationships became stronger, and my work flourished as I aligned it with what I loved.

Through this journey, I discovered just how crucial self-reflection is. Taking the time to look inward allowed me to understand my thoughts and feelings better. I learned to identify patterns in my behavior and recognize what truly matters to me. This awareness helped me make more intentional choices, guiding me toward an authentic and fulfilling life.

Staying connected to the world around me became equally important. I realized that engaging with others and nature deepens my sense of belonging. Whether it's sharing a laugh with a friend, enjoying a walk in the park, or simply appreciating a beautiful sunset, these moments remind me that I'm part of something bigger. They inspire me and fill me with positivity.

As I embraced God's frequency and deepened my spiritual practice, I found myself navigating life with greater ease and clarity. This alignment brought me peace and opened doors to new opportunities I had never imagined before.

One significant opportunity arose when I began working for a nonprofit dedicated to helping veterans, which was launching a new campus in the metroplex. In this vibrant environment, filled with purpose and compassion, I met a radiant woman who walked in for an interview. I was the first person to greet her, and from the moment we connected, I sensed something calm and refreshing about her spirit. Her presence was like a gentle breeze, uplifting and invigorating, and it sparked an immediate sense of connection between us.

Over the next year, our friendship blossomed organically. We spent countless hours together at work, sharing stories and supporting each other in our respective healing journeys. Both of us were recovering from intense breakups, and we appreciated the understanding we found in each other. We were mindful about not wanting to "rebound date," instead focusing on building a strong, platonic foundation.

During this time, I felt incredibly centered and balanced. My chakras aligned with the Universe, and this state of equilibrium allowed me to approach our friendship openly and authentically. I was free from the weight of past relationships, and it felt refreshing to connect with someone on such a genuine level. Our conversations flowed easily, often delving into our dreams, aspirations, and even our fears.

This friendship became a safe space for both of us to share our vulnerabilities without judgment. It was a time of growth, not just for me but for both of us, as we supported each other in navigating the complexities of healing and self-discovery. Little did I know that this bond would enrich my life and serve as a stepping stone for deeper connections and experiences.

In Hinduism and yoga, chakras are psych-energetic centers in the human body that channel a subtle energy, helping the mind, organs, and intellect function at their best. These energy centers play a crucial role in maintaining balance and harmony within us, and I was determined to stay in this optimal state for as long as I could. However, the Universe had other plans in store for me.

After we both moved on from the nonprofit, life took us in different directions, and we lost touch for a while. Though I cherished the time we spent together, I understood that sometimes, the ebb and flow of life leads us away from certain connections. I continued to focus on my spiritual practice and personal growth, but a part of me missed the refreshing energy and deep conversations we had shared.

Several months later, as if guided by a hidden force, our paths crossed again one fateful night at a local jazz club. The atmosphere was electric, filled with the smooth sounds of music that seemed to wrap around us like a warm embrace. That night, a kind of magnetic force was in the air, pulling us toward each other once more.

As I entered the club, I felt an inexplicable pull, almost like the universe conspired to reunite us. When our eyes met across the room, it was as if time stood still. The connection we had felt before came rushing back, stronger than ever, igniting a sense of familiarity and comfort. We exchanged smiles, and I could sense that we were both equally surprised and delighted by this unexpected encounter.

I can remember it like it was yesterday—how we spent the entire night making out in a dark corner of the club, surrounded by the smooth sounds of neo-soul music. It felt magical like the world around us had faded away.

After officially dating, I worked up the courage to propose to her on our one-year anniversary. I initially realized that my desire to marry her was driven by a fear of change. I was scared of what might happen if I didn't take that step. But as I thought more about it, I understood that marrying her was truly the best decision I ever made.

Jennifer was different from anyone I had ever met. She was the first person who really understood me—every part of me, even the messy bits. With her, I felt I could be completely honest, sharing my thoughts and fears without holding back. She wasn't just my lover; she was my wife, my best friend, and my moral compass.

Jennifer had this amazing ability to bring out the best in me and always kept me honest. She had a way of seeing my potential, even when I couldn't see it myself. Whenever I felt stuck or unsure, she was right there, encouraging me to push through the doubts. Her belief in me was like a light, guiding me toward my dreams.

Sometimes, I would talk about ideas or goals, but they felt so far away, like distant stars. Jennifer would listen intently, her eyes shining with excitement. She would gently nudge me to take that first step, reminding me that every big dream starts with a small action. Her encouragement made me believe I could chase after things I had only daydreamed about before.

With her by my side, I felt stronger and more capable than ever before. I found myself taking risks I never thought I would. Whether pursuing a new job, starting a creative project, or even stepping out of my comfort zone socially, Jennifer was my constant support.

Every time I achieved something, no matter how small, I wanted to share it with her because she had played a huge part in that success.

Every moment with her reminded me that I was loved for who I truly was, flaws and all. In her presence, I felt safe to be myself, to share my hopes and fears without fear of judgment. Her laughter and warmth filled my days, making even the toughest moments easier to handle. I knew that I could face anything with Jennifer, which made all the difference in my life.

From that night on, we went on to share nine amazing years together before her untimely passing; shortly after we returned from a trip to Africa, where we delved deeper into my Yoruba cultural heritage. Those years were filled with laughter, love, and countless memories that I cherish every day.

Jennifer was incredibly beautiful, not just in her appearance but in the way she carried herself. Her smile could light up the darkest room, and her energy commanded attention whenever she walked in. It was impossible not to be drawn to her warmth and kindness. She had this natural ability to make everyone around her feel special, and her laughter was like music that lifted my spirits.

She was my soulmate, twin flame, and best friend, all wrapped into one. With her, I felt a connection that went beyond words, a bond that seemed to intertwine our very souls. We shared everything—our dreams, our fears, and our silly inside jokes. I often called her my "Brown Sugar," a term that perfectly captured her sweetness and the richness she brought to my life.

Our adventures together were countless, from exploring new places to quiet nights at home just enjoying each other's company. We would spend hours talking about life, culture, and our future. Each day felt like a gift, filled with love and understanding.

Losing her was like losing a part of myself. The world felt different without her bright light, but our love continues to inspire me. I hold onto our memories tightly, knowing she will always be a part of who I am. Jennifer taught me to embrace life, to chase my dreams, and to love deeply. And for that, I am forever grateful.

I honestly can't recall one major argument we ever had in those nine years. This was largely due to our deep commitment to truthful communication—not just honesty, but a more profound connection where we truly expressed our feelings. We understood that honesty alone wasn't enough; it was about creating a safe space to share our thoughts openly.

There were no secrets between us. Nothing was off-limits for discussion, no matter how uncomfortable the topic might seem. We believed it was essential to speak our minds and share how we really felt without holding back. Whether it was about our dreams, fears, or even the little annoyances that could build up over time, we tackled everything head-on.

Our only rule was simple: no one would get upset. We agreed that we could maturely talk through any issue. If emotions started rising, we would take a step back and breathe, ensuring that the conversation remained constructive rather than becoming heated.

This approach allowed us to resolve conflicts before they could fester, building a stronger bond in the process.

It was incredibly refreshing to know that we could share our feelings without fear of judgment. This open dialogue helped us understand each other on a deeper level. We celebrated our successes together and comforted each other during tough times, always knowing we were a team.

This foundation of honest communication kept our relationship strong and made our love grow deeper. I think that's why, even in moments of tension, we never lost sight of our respect and affection for one another. We genuinely valued each other's perspectives, and mutual respect allowed us to navigate any challenges life threw our way.

I often heard other married people say, "Marriage is work," "Marriage is give and take," "Marriage is grown folk business," and "Marriage has its challenges." However, we had a different experience because we prioritized effective communication and transparency from the beginning. Neither of us felt pressured in our marriage; instead, we cultivated a partnership built on trust and understanding.

In year three or four of our relationship, we shared the concept of exploring a polyamorous triad. It felt like a natural extension of our open dialogue, a chance to deepen our connection while embracing the possibility of loving others. We approached it not as a challenge but as an opportunity for growth, both individually and together. Our discussions were honest and respectful, allowing us to navigate the complexities confidently.

Through this journey, we discovered that love isn't a finite resource; it can expand in ways we never expected.

Each new relationship brought fresh perspectives and experiences, enriching our own bond. We learned to celebrate each other's joys and support each other through any difficulties.

Our approach to marriage—focused on communication, respect, and exploration—had turned what many see as hard work into a joyful adventure. Instead of feeling like a burden, our relationship had become a beautiful mix of connections, full of love and understanding. This allowed us to grow both together and as individuals.

I had always known she was bisexual, and we would occasionally invite another woman into our relationship to date together. This non-traditional dynamic isn't for everyone, yet it shouldn't be frowned upon by those who preferred a traditional monogamous relationship. What matters most is that you and your partner decide what works best for your relationship.

The key to a successful relationship or marriage lay in being truthful about our intentions and honest about what we truly wanted. We took the time to communicate openly about our desires and boundaries, ensuring that everyone involved felt comfortable and respected. It was about creating a safe space to explore our feelings without judgment.

If the person you meet doesn't share your preferences, it's better to move on rather than live a lie. Too many people stay in situationships out of fear of being alone, convincing themselves that compromise is the only option. But sometimes, being alone is what is best for both parties, allowing space for growth and self-discovery.

As I mentioned earlier, it took me being alone for over a year—embracing celibacy and focusing on my inner peace—before I was truly ready to find my soulmate.

During that time, I learned to connect with myself more deeply. I explored my passions, reflected on my values, and better understood what I wanted in a partner. This period of solitude wasn't always easy, but it was necessary for my personal growth.

When I finally opened myself up to love again, I felt more grounded and aligned with my true self. I realized that being single allowed me to cultivate a strong foundation, making it possible to recognize the right person when they came along. By prioritizing my happiness and clarity, I was better equipped to enter a relationship that resonated with me.

Ultimately, taking the time to understand myself led to a more fulfilling and authentic connection when I found my soulmate.

"Brown Sugar," a beloved favorite of mine, kicks off its storyline on my birthday, July 18, but in 1984. This setting adds a special layer of nostalgia for me, as it captures the essence of hip-hop's early days, a time filled with creativity and cultural transformation. The film explores the deep connection between love and music, paralleling the rhythms of life with the beats of the era.

Chapter 6: One Day You're Here and the Next...

As the New Year approached, we continued our cherished tradition of celebrating with an international trip, and this year, we chose Accra, Ghana, as our destination. The excitement in the air was palpable, a buzzing mix of anticipation and hope as we reflected on the goals we had set for ourselves—ambitions we were determined to achieve by the end of 2023.

With its vibrant culture, rich history, and warm hospitality, Accra felt like the perfect backdrop for our New Year's celebration. As we boarded the plane, we couldn't help but share our dreams and aspirations for the year ahead.

Each of us has personal goals: some pursue career advancement, while others aim for personal growth or deeper connections with loved ones. We made a pact to support each other in these endeavors, just as we had done in previous years.

Upon arrival, the lively streets of Accra greeted us with open arms. The hustle and bustle, the colorful markets, and the aroma of traditional dishes wafting through the air filled us with a sense of adventure.

We spent our first days exploring the city's landmarks, from the poignant Kwame Nkrumah Mausoleum to the vibrant arts district of Osu. Every corner seemed to pulse with energy and inspiration, reinforcing our resolve to make the most of our year.

As we immersed ourselves in the local culture, we found ourselves captivated by the stories of resilience and hope surrounding us. Conversations with locals sparked new ideas and perspectives, reminding us of the importance of community and connection in achieving our goals.

We participated in a traditional dance workshop, laughed at our clumsy attempts to mimic the fluid movements, and felt an exhilarating sense of freedom from stepping outside our comfort zones.

On New Year's Eve, we gathered on the beach, the sound of waves crashing against the shore blending with distant drumming. Under a blanket of stars, we reflected on our experiences and shared our resolutions for the coming year. The ocean breeze carried our hopes into the night, and as the clock struck midnight, we cheered together, welcoming a new year and a renewed commitment to ourselves and each other.

With hearts full of joy and determination, we set off into 2023, ready to turn our dreams into reality, buoyed by the spirit of Accra and the bonds we had strengthened during our unforgettable trip.

On a typical Monday morning in January, I rose before the sun, embracing the quiet stillness of the early hours. My routine kicked off with a vigorous workout on the Peloton, pushing my limits as I cycled through challenging terrains and engaging in high-energy sessions.

Following that, I hit the gym, like I always do, for strength training or an invigorating boxing class. These workouts were not just a way to stay fit; they were a crucial part of my daily ritual, setting a positive tone for the rest of the day and reinforcing my commitment to the goals I had envisioned for the year ahead.

As I finished my workout, my wife was just waking up, her sleepy eyes lighting up as she caught sight of me. After exchanging our customary morning kiss, I asked her if she would like to go out for dinner that evening.

She responded with an elegant smile, her eyes sparkling with excitement, and said, “I look forward to it, my husband.” That simple moment filled me with joy, and I couldn't help but carry that happiness throughout the day.

Time seemed to fly as I moved through my tasks, but the smile on my face never faded. The anticipation of spending the evening with one of the most remarkable women in the world kept my spirits high. When the evening finally arrived, we headed to a local high-end steakhouse known for its warm ambience and exquisite cuisine.

As we settled in, the atmosphere buzzed with laughter and conversation. We were soon joined at the bar by another couple, and before long, we found ourselves engaged in delightful banter. The evening unfolded with clinking glasses, shared stories, and hearty laughs, creating an unforgettable connection with our new friends.

The food was divine, each bite more satisfying than the last, but the joy of the moment and the warmth of my wife's presence made the night truly special. We left the restaurant feeling even closer, our hearts full and our spirits lifted by the shared experiences of the evening.

On the ride home, we filled the car with our usual sing-along and laughter, the kind of easy banter that made even the shortest trips feel like mini-adventures. She was particularly playful, tossing out silly jokes and singing off-key to her favorite songs. Just before we pulled into the driveway, she casually mentioned, "I'm feeling a little light-headed." I didn't think much of it; maybe it was just the lingering effects of a long day.

Once we pulled up, I grabbed my bag and headed inside, the sound of her laughter still echoing in my mind. I walked into the closet to change clothes, the comforting routine momentarily distracting me. But then, a chilling realization crept in—I hadn't heard her voice in a while. I paused, the silence wrapping around me like a heavy blanket, and a knot of unease formed in my stomach.

Stepping into the foyer, I called out to her, but the stillness swallowed my words. My heart raced as I turned the corner, and that's when I saw her. She lay on the floor, motionless, her eyes closed, and my world seemed to tilt on its axis. I rushed to her side, panic surging through me. "Honey!" I shouted, kneeling beside her, desperately hoping for a response that wouldn't come.

I checked for a pulse, my hands trembling as I searched for the steady rhythm that defined our lives together. Nothing. The reality of the moment crashed over me like a wave, the laughter from just minutes ago feeling like a cruel memory. I was lost, the air thick with dread, and all I could think was how fragile everything felt, how quickly joy could transform into fear.

I fumbled for my phone, my hands shaking as I dialed for help, each second stretching painfully long. At that moment, time stood still, and all I could do was hope that I'd hear her voice again, that this was just a nightmare from which I would wake. But deep down, I knew something had changed irrevocably, and the fear that gripped my heart was unlike anything I had ever known.

Once she came to her senses, a moment of relief washed over me. I thought maybe everything was going to be okay after all. But just as quickly as that hope emerged, it was shattered when she suddenly started to seize, her body trembling violently before collapsing back onto the floor. My heart dropped as I rushed to her side, fear gripping me like a vice.

In a panic, I grabbed my phone and called 911, my voice shaky as I explained the situation. The operator's calm instructions cut through the chaos: "Start CPR until the First Responders arrive."

My hands trembled as I knelt beside her, desperately trying to remember the training I had once taken so long ago. I pressed down on her chest, counting each compression, urging her to come back to me, praying for a miracle.

Time felt distorted as I worked on her, every second stretching into what felt like an eternity. It was a blur of adrenaline and fear, punctuated only by the sound of my heartbeat thundering in my ears.

The paramedics arrived within what felt like moments, but my focus was solely on her. They took over, moving with precision and urgency as they assessed her condition and prepared to transport her.

They worked in the middle of our living room for ten long minutes, their voices blending commands and reassurance. I stood nearby, helpless, watching as they fought to stabilize her, their determination a stark contrast to my sense of dread. Finally, they carefully lifted her onto a stretcher, and I felt a mix of relief and panic wash over me as they wheeled her out of our home and into the waiting ambulance. I clung to the hope that she would be okay, even as my world felt unraveling around me.

As I followed the ambulance on that short, two-minute drive to the nearby hospital, a heavy realization settled in the back of my mind: my wife was nearing her transition. Even in that fleeting moment, I felt a sense of dread, something I couldn't shake.

The image of her lying on the living room floor haunted me, especially the emptiness in her eyes—they seemed to stare into nothingness, devoid of the warmth and spirit I had known for so long. I felt as though her soul had already begun to drift away, leaving behind a shell of the woman I loved.

Within an hour later, my worst fears were confirmed—my wife passed away from an arterial embolism, a blood clot that had taken her from me far too soon.

Ironically, it was the same hospital where, just a few years earlier, my mother had triumphed over breast cancer, celebrating her last treatment by ringing the bell of victory. The stark contrast of those two experiences hit me hard: joy and loss intertwined in a way I could never have anticipated.

The number 23 would take on a different meaning for me as the year progressed, its significance unfolding in unexpected ways. Number 23 holds significance in various contexts, including religious and cultural symbolism.

In the context of the Quran, specifically Surah Al-Mu'minun (Chapter 23), the verses discuss themes of creation, human existence, and the ultimate return to God, which ties into broader concepts of life and death.

Verse 23:23 emphasizes the oneness of Allah and calls for worship, suggesting that recognizing God's sovereignty can lead to a deeper understanding of life, death, and accountability in the afterlife. The mention of "fear Him" underscores the importance of reverence and consciousness of one's actions, particularly in the face of mortality.

In broader interpretations, the number 23 has been linked to mortality in some cultures, often viewed through numerology or mystical frameworks. For example, it can be associated with the idea of human life cycles, as 23 years is often a transitional period in many societies.

The interplay of these ideas invites reflection on how the recognition of a higher power and the inevitability of death shape moral and spiritual values. Understanding one's purpose and the transient nature of life can lead to deeper faith and worship fulfillment, as the Quran encourages.

At that moment, however, all I could feel was an overwhelming sense of emptiness, the weight of grief pressing down on me like a heavy shroud. I had lost not just my partner but a part of myself, and the road ahead felt uncertain and daunting.

As the doctor's words echoed in my mind, I felt a heavy weight settle in my chest. It was as if the air had thickened, making it hard to breathe. I stumbled back to the waiting room, my legs barely holding me up, and instinctively reached for my phone.

My fingers trembled as I typed a message to my mom and sister. The words felt foreign as I wrote, "She's gone. I don't know what to do." I hit send and stared at the screen, waiting for their responses like a lifeline, yet knowing that nothing they could say would alleviate the suffocating despair that engulfed me.

Next, I dialed my best friend's number, my heart racing as I waited for him to pick up. When his voice finally came through, it sounded distant and muffled. I struggled to form coherent sentences; the words tangled in my throat.

"I… I need you," I managed to say, feeling the tears finally spill over. His immediate concern was palpable, but I couldn't focus on the comfort he offered. I was trapped in a whirlwind of emotions—anger, disbelief, sadness—each one crashing over me like a relentless wave.

As I sat there in the cold, sterile room, I felt utterly alone, even in the presence of those who loved me. Grief wrapped around me like a shroud, and I couldn't shake the overwhelming feeling of being unmoored. The world outside continued as if nothing had changed, while my own universe had shattered, leaving only fragments of memories and an aching void.

I don't even remember how much time passed as I lay next to her cold body in the hospital bed. The sterile smell of the room mixed with the overwhelming silence, and I fought against the disbelief that gripped me.

It was difficult to accept that someone who had been my best friend, lover, and wife for the past decade was gone. We had experienced our share of ups and downs initially. Still, as time passed, we learned to navigate life's challenges together, feeling the invisible forces of the universe drawing us closer.

We had built a life rich with memories, laughter, and love, and now it all felt like it was slipping away. I struggled to reconcile the vibrant woman I had known with the stillness beside me.

Each passing moment deepened the ache in my heart, and I longed for one more smile, shared joke, or moment of connection.

In that sterile room, surrounded by machines and the echo of footsteps in the hallway, I was faced with an unfathomable void, and the weight of grief felt almost unbearable.

"One day, while reminiscing, I found myself reflecting on "One Day" by UGK, one of our favorite hip-hop groups. Their music had always been a source of connection for us, and this particular track resonated deeply, evoking memories of the moments we shared together. The lyrics, filled with hope and reflection, took me back to the laughter and the countless late-night conversations where we bonded over our love for their music."

Chapter 7: The Power of 23 and Spiritually Woke

The *Principia Discordia* introduces the number 23 as a key corollary to the Law of Fives, which posits that "all things happen in fives, or are divisible by or are multiples of five, or are somehow directly or indirectly appropriate to 5." Within this framework, 23 emerges as a number that embodies this law's peculiar nature, appearing in various unexpected or seemingly coincidental ways.

Its significance extends beyond mere numerology, suggesting a deeper, almost mystical pattern that hints at hidden connections in the world around us. For followers of Discordianism, 23 symbolizes the disruption of conventional order and the revelation of a deeper chaos underlying reality.

In the realm of angel numbers, repeating sequences like 2323 hold even greater meaning. When a number is repeated, it amplifies the original vibration and essence of the digits involved, acting as a kind of energetic magnifier.

Such patterns carry urgent or heightened messages from the spiritual realm, encouraging us to pay closer attention to the energies influencing our lives. The repetition draws our awareness to key themes and areas that need our conscious engagement, prompting us to look beyond the surface and recognize the symbolic messages at play.

When the number 23 repeats as 2323, its impact is intensified, as if the universe is emphasizing a point that cannot be ignored. This numerical pattern serves as a celestial highlighter, directing our focus to the areas of life that require deliberate attention, such as personal growth, relationships, or pursuing one's life purpose.

It is a call to align with the flow of life, to notice where shifts are happening, and to trust that these changes, even if they seem chaotic, are guiding us toward a higher state of awareness and balance.

The appearance of 2323 suggests that we are being urged to awaken to new perspectives, embrace the unexpected, and find meaning in the seemingly random occurrences that unfold. It encourages a mindset that sees synchronicity not as mere coincidence but as a form of divine communication.

By tuning into these signs, we can gain valuable insights, enabling us to respond to life's challenges and opportunities with greater clarity and purpose. This connection between the number and life events shows that life isn't just random; there's a hidden order guiding us.

The date I enlisted in the U.S. military was 3/23; coincidentally, the day I officially retired due to medical reasons was also 3/23. It's a powerful reminder that signs from the universe are always around us, appearing when we're open to seeing them. My wife's death was officially recorded on 1/23/23 at 12:23 am, too.

These patterns and synchronicities often appear as subtle nudges from the universe, guiding us toward a deeper understanding of our journey and purpose. They're like whispers in the background, signaling that we're on the right path—or prompting us to adjust our course when we're not.

Consider the old turn-dial car radios that came standard in vehicles up until the mid-90s. You had to adjust the dial carefully, tuning into just the right frequency to get a clear signal. If you were even slightly off, the station would be filled with static or distorted sounds.

But when you hit the sweet spot, the signal would come through clearly, delivering the music or message as intended. Similarly, the universe communicates with us through signs and synchronicities, but we must be attuned to the right "frequency" in our own lives to pick up on them.

When we notice repeating numbers, meaningful dates, or other patterns, it's as if we're catching glimpses of a deeper, underlying order that's always there, even if we don't consciously recognize it. These signs act as guideposts, directing us to pay closer attention to the areas of life that require our focus or need adjustment.

Being attuned to these subtle signals means cultivating an awareness beyond the surface level, allowing us to perceive connections and meanings that may otherwise go unnoticed. It's about recognizing the harmony in what may seem like random events and understanding that these moments often align with our personal growth, purpose, and spiritual evolution.

The fact that both pivotal dates in my military career fell on 3/23 feels like more than coincidence—it feels like a cosmic acknowledgment, a signpost reminding me of the path I've walked.

Back in the day, if you were far from a radio station's broadcast, you couldn't just leave the dial where it was—you had to make fine adjustments to catch the signal or use a more powerful antenna to get a clear reception. This principle isn't limited to radio waves; it also applies to tuning into the deeper frequencies of the universe, such as angel numbers, premonitions, dream interpretations, or even experiencing déjà vu.

One must cultivate a focused and disciplined mind to access these subtle energies and powers, much like fine-tuning the radio dial. It requires intention, consistent practice, and, most importantly, minimizing distractions that can cloud our perception.

Both of my grandmothers had a saying: "An idle mind is the Devil's playground." They taught me that if you're not filling your mind with meaningful and productive activities, you leave room for negativity and unproductive habits to take root.

Their old-school wisdom emphasized the importance of keeping one's mind active and directed toward worthy pursuits, a philosophy that shaped my gumption and resilience over time.

Through their teachings, I learned to recognize the value of mental discipline, which is essential for accessing deeper insights and understanding the signs that life presents. This upbringing instilled in me a commitment to self-improvement and a refusal to let idleness undermine my growth. Just as a radio needs the right adjustments to receive a signal from far away, we, too, need to fine-tune our inner focus to connect with the universal energies that guide us.

This process involves training the mind, setting aside distractions, and staying aligned with our higher purpose. The strength and determination I gained during my adolescence years help shaped me into the person I am today, empowering me to navigate life with clarity and purpose.

These teachings focused heavily on working hard and keeping your faith. As I was exposed to different countries and cultures, I learned the true power of cultivating a mindset that seeks meaning in everyday experiences and uses those moments to grow. Through this continuous process of fine-tuning our awareness, we can connect with the universe's subtle messages and tap into the insights that can guide our lives.

This idea of recognizing patterns extends to the concept of angel numbers, considered messages from the divine realm sent to offer love, light, and guidance on our life journey.

During my study of numerology, I learned that each digit from 1 to 9 carries its unique significance. When these numbers appear in sequence, they convey deeper meanings meant to help us navigate our daily lives with greater understanding and purpose.

Angel numbers serve as subtle reminders from the universe, prompting us to pay attention to particular aspects of our lives and offering reassurance and direction when we need it most.

Spiritual Growth: The appearance of the number 23 signals the beginning of a new path on your spiritual journey. It suggests that a gateway opens, leading you toward a deeper understanding of yourself and the world around you. This number arrives as a reminder that spiritual awakenings often take different forms and can arise from joyful and difficult experiences.

In fact, many profound spiritual shifts are born out of challenging times, when life's trials push us to seek higher truths and uncover inner wisdom. Seeing the number 23 may indicate that you are on the brink of such a breakthrough, where growth is not only possible but destined.

A Call to Help Others: Alongside its message of spiritual evolution, the number 23 also represents a call to service. It encourages you to use your gifts, experiences, and insights to uplift those around you. This angelic message suggests that the path to your growth is intertwined with helping others.

By reaching out to offer love, support, and guidance, you not only contribute positively to the lives of others but also elevate your own spiritual vibration. It is a reminder that true fulfillment comes from living with purpose and sharing your light with the world.

Transformation: The presence of the number 23 highlights the inevitability of change and its transformative power. Transformation is often uncomfortable, as it involves shedding old patterns, beliefs, or ways of life to make way for something new. Yet, this number reassures you that such changes are necessary for your evolution.

It invites you to trust the process and see these shifts as part of a divine plan that is guiding you toward your highest potential. When the number 23 appears, it signals embracing transformation with an open heart, knowing it will lead you closer to your true self.

Overall, angel number 23 serves as a beacon, urging you to stay attuned to the signs the universe is sending and to take conscious steps forward on your spiritual path. It brings a message of hope, reminding you that every challenge holds the seed of growth, every act of kindness strengthens your connection to the divine, and every change is an opportunity to transform your life in beautiful and meaningful ways.

For me, the number 23 became profoundly significant after the sudden loss of my wife. I was there when she took her last breath, right in the home we had lovingly built together. The memory still haunts me—finding her collapsed and unresponsive in the foyer; I keep replaying the moment, thinking I should have rushed her to the hospital immediately. The weight of that decision, or lack of action, is something I continue to carry.

Her passing marked the beginning of a new chapter in my life, one focused on "Helping Others." Over the past two years, I've encountered strangers in the most ordinary places—a restaurant bar, a car wash waiting room, or a golf course. These meetings have become almost like divine appointments, moments where sharing my story as a widower has had a meaningful impact on others. It's as though my experiences are not just for me to endure but to use in helping those who are struggling.

In sharing my journey, I've been able to assist in surprising ways. I helped save the marriages of two close friends by encouraging them to see beyond their differences and recognize how small their issues were in the grand scheme of things. I've mentored a high school senior, offering guidance during a pivotal moment in his life.

And more recently, I met a man at the golf course who had lost his son to suicide a few years before. Our connection was immediate, and since meeting him 23 days after my wife's passing, we've become close friends, supporting each other as we navigate our separate but deeply intertwined grief.

These encounters have become more than just random moments; they feel like part of a greater plan. I've found purpose in my pain by opening up and being vulnerable. Sharing my story isn't just about revisiting the past but about transforming loss into a force for good.

Whether it's providing comfort to someone who feels alone in their struggles, offering perspective to save a relationship, or simply being a compassionate listener, I've discovered that in helping others, I'm also healing myself.

The relationships and bonds formed through these experiences are profound, demonstrating that there can be light even in our darkest moments. My connections have shown me that we can find purpose and growth through tragedy and that by giving of ourselves, we receive far more than we ever anticipated. It's a continuous reminder that we're all connected in our struggles, and sometimes, a simple act of sharing can create a ripple effect that reaches far beyond what we can see.

The number 23 carries a unique blend of energies that can propel us toward a higher state of being. It serves as a reminder that real transformation isn't instantaneous—it's a process that unfolds over time and requires dedication.

Achieving this elevated state means embracing the discipline necessary to tap into the Powers of the Universe, which are always within reach for those willing to undergo the journey of transformation, or as some might call it, an ascension to an untapped mental state. When we commit to this path, we open ourselves up to limitless possibilities, allowing us to transcend the ordinary and unlock our true potential.

The key to harnessing the power of transformation lies in mastering three essential practices: channeling our emotions, centering our thoughts, and quieting our minds. Each of these requires effort and persistence, but they also pave the way for profound inner growth.

The most challenging of the three is often learning to channel our emotions effectively—taking charge of our emotional responses rather than letting them dictate our actions. It's about developing the ability to acknowledge our feelings without being overwhelmed by them, using our emotional energy as a source of strength rather than turmoil.

Channeling our emotions is a skill that allows us to transform negative energy into a force for positive change. Instead of being controlled by anger, fear, or sadness, we learn to harness these feelings and direct them constructively. This practice is not about suppressing emotions but understanding them and using that understanding to fuel growth. It requires a deep level of self-awareness and the willingness to confront and process difficult feelings head-on.

Centering our thoughts is the next step in this transformative process. It involves developing a focused mindset where our attention is directed toward what truly matters rather than being scattered by distractions.

When we learn to center our thoughts, we can navigate life's challenges with clarity and purpose, allowing us to stay grounded even when circumstances become overwhelming. This discipline enables us to align our actions with our intentions, making us more effective in pursuing our goals.

Finally, quieting the mind is about achieving a state of inner stillness where the constant chatter of thoughts begins to subside. This is not an easy feat in a world filled with noise and distractions, but it is essential for accessing deeper levels of consciousness and tuning into the subtle signals of the universe. When the mind is quiet, we create space for intuition and insight to emerge, enabling us to connect more fully with our higher selves and the universal energies at play.

The transformation journey through these practices leads to a more profound understanding of who we are and what we are capable of. It's an ongoing process, a commitment to continuous growth, and a willingness to embrace change with an open heart. We begin to realize that transformation is not just about changing who we are but about revealing the boundless potential that has always existed within us.

When we come to understand that emotions are not "figuratively real," in the sense that they don't have to control us, we gain the power to shift them in ways that work to our advantage. Emotions are real experiences, but they don't have to dictate our responses or outcomes. This realization allows us to reframe our emotional states and direct them toward growth, healing, or action.

Proverbs 23:23 advises us to *"buy the truth, and do not sell it; wisdom, instruction, and insight as well."* This verse invites us to reflect deeply on our priorities and choices throughout life's journey. It asks us to consider what we truly value, reminding us that pursuing wisdom and understanding is far more important than material gains.

For me, the number 23 became a powerful symbol that seemed to appear everywhere—almost like it was slapping me in the face, urging me to pay attention. But in the initial months following my wife's passing, I was too consumed by grief to recognize the signs that were all around me.

Like anyone who experiences the devastating loss of a spouse or significant other, I found myself questioning, "Why did this happen to me?" I wrestled with the idea that maybe the universe was exacting some kind of karmic debt for my past transgressions, cashing in on what felt like years of happiness and success. Life had been going remarkably well; financially, we were comfortable with multiple streams of income that eliminated most concerns about money. We enjoyed luxurious trips, lived in beautiful homes that were far too big for just two people, and indulged in "because I can" purchases that we considered fruit for our labor.

In the aftermath of my wife's passing, I couldn't help but wonder if this was all a wake-up call, a lesson from God telling me to "dial it back." Perhaps the luxury and abundance had distracted me from deeper truths, pulling my focus away from what truly matters. It was as if I needed to be reminded that life's blessings are not to be taken for granted and that excess without purpose could cloud my sense of gratitude and meaning.

The loss forced me to confront the uncomfortable reality that no amount of wealth or material comfort could shield me from pain. It became a powerful catalyst for re-evaluating my life, priorities, and how I lived. Was I too caught up in pursuing things that brought temporary pleasure while overlooking the more enduring values of love, faith, and connection? The signs were there, but in the fog of grief, they were initially obscured, only to become clearer as I worked through the pain.

Gradually, I began to see that the number 23 wasn't just a random occurrence—it was a message calling me to realign my life. It reminded me to seek deeper wisdom, be more mindful of my choices, and understand that even when life seems to be going perfectly, we should never lose sight of the spiritual truths that keep us grounded. The number invited me to reflect on the balance between abundance and humility, success and simplicity. It was a call to redirect my focus from outward achievements to inner growth, from material wealth to spiritual richness.

In the process, I learned that transformation often emerges from our darkest moments. It's not just about surviving loss but about using the experience as a powerful force for positive change.

And in that sense, 23 became more than just a number—it became a symbol of the lessons I needed to learn, the wisdom I was invited to seek, and the path I was meant to follow as I rebuilt my life with renewed purpose.

I often said, "It was my turn," as if life had finally dealt me a bad hand. When my wife passed away suddenly, it felt like a reminder that no one is immune to suffering; we all face our share of hardships. It was my time to be tested, and I had to endure a painful chapter that would change everything I thought I knew.

The number 23 appears in the Bible with significance tied to God's sovereignty and judgment, symbolizing accountability, transformation, and divine purpose. It marks individuals set apart for a specific role, reminding us that a higher order is at play even in chaos or injustice. In the New Testament, 23 also connects to resurrection and new beginnings, symbolizing the transition from suffering to redemption and the power to rise after trials.

In numerology, 23 reflects change and progress, with 2 and 3 equaling 5, a number associated with freedom and growth. It serves as an invitation to embrace transformation, explore new horizons, and trust in the unfolding journey.

The recurring presence of 23 became a sign of divine order in my life, urging me to see my struggles not as arbitrary but as part of a greater plan—an opportunity for growth and spiritual awakening, even in the darkest times.

"The power of 23 often symbolizes change, transformation, and innovation. It represents a blend of stability (2) and creativity (3), often associated with breakthroughs and unexpected shifts."

Chapter 8: Life After Death

After my wife passed, I could have easily withdrawn from the world—isolating myself in the bedroom, hiding under the covers, crying endlessly, and neglecting my health. It would have been the path of least resistance, letting the overwhelming weight of grief pull me under.

In that space, it felt as though nothing mattered; the world had lost its color and meaning. Days blurred into nights, and it seemed easier to give in to the numbness, to let myself slowly waste away. After all, what was the point of trying to continue when everything I had loved and hoped for seemed to have vanished along with her?

But I knew, deep down, that surrendering to that urge wouldn't bring peace. It wouldn't heal the gaping wound in my heart nor would it honor the love we had shared. If I allowed myself to be consumed by despair, what would I have left to offer to those still around me—the people who still needed me, even if I felt broken inside? And what would my wife have wanted for me? Certainly not this.

Over the next year, I went through a whirlwind of emotions—grief, anger, sadness, despair, confusion, guilt, loneliness, regret, fear, frustration, disbelief, and even brief glimpses of hope that felt almost cruel. Each day brought a new set of highs and lows, like riding an emotional rollercoaster.

There were times when the grief was so overwhelming it felt like a crushing weight on my chest, draining every bit of strength I had. Anger would suddenly flare up, leaving me bitter and questioning the fairness of it all. Sadness became familiar, waiting in the background, ready to drag me down whenever I thought I was regaining some stability. It was like being caught in the grip of invisible forces, pushing and pulling me in every direction, no matter how hard I tried to resist.

I wanted to believe that with time or enough effort, I could rise above these feelings, but the logical part of my brain failed to convince the rest of me.

At times, I felt utterly powerless, as if I were drowning in emotions that I couldn't see or touch but were nonetheless suffocating. They consumed me, leaving me paralyzed, unable to think clearly or function in the way I used to.

It was during this relentless battle with my emotions that I found myself turning to alcohol more frequently. What started as an occasional drink to take the edge off soon became a nightly ritual. Alcohol became my crutch, the only thing that seemed to dull the pain, to mute the constant noise of grief and sorrow that I couldn't escape.

It numbed everything, and for those brief moments, I could forget. But the more I drank, the more disconnected I became—from myself, from others, from reality.

My appetite faded completely; food no longer mattered. The simple joy of a meal disappeared, replaced by a numb indifference. I didn't feel hunger, just emptiness.

Each morning felt like climbing a mountain. I would lie in bed, staring at the ceiling, wrestling with the weight of getting up. The world outside continued to move at its normal pace, indifferent to the fact that my world had stopped the day I lost my wife.

Responsibilities didn't disappear just because I had become a widower. There were still bills to pay, people to see, conversations to have, and a life to live—even when mine felt like it had come to a standstill. Putting on a mask each day, pretending I could carry on as before, became an exhausting routine. The days blurred together, a constant struggle between hiding my pain from the world and battling it alone in the quiet moments when no one else was watching.

Every day, as part of my routine, I made time for prayer and meditation in my backyard, a small moment of solace amid the chaos of grief. I always made sure to face East. This wasn't just a random choice but deeply symbolic for me. First, it aligned with my Islamic beliefs, a practice that brought me comfort and connection to my faith during such a difficult time. Second, it was about what the East represents.

The sun rises in the East and sets in the West. For me, this daily ritual of watching the sun begin its journey was a reminder of the cycle of life. No matter how dark the night had been, the sun would always rise again. I needed to emulate that. I had to find a way to rise each day, despite the pain, despite the loss, and continue moving forward.

The sun's steady, unwavering presence symbolized hope and resilience. It sustains all life, and I, too, had to find a way to be a source of strength—not just for myself but for those around me. Like the sun, I had to rise, endure, and give light, even when everything inside me felt dark. This mindset slowly became my anchor, guiding me through the darkest days and reminding me that, like the sun, I could find the strength to keep going.

My wife's passing was a profound wake-up call, forcing me to make significant adjustments in how I approached my daily life. It was a stark reminder of how much she contributed to the rhythm of our household and how deeply intertwined our lives had been.

She had always supported me in my entrepreneurial pursuits, allowing me to dive into my business ventures, whether in real estate or IT consulting. While I focused on work, she took charge of the home, effortlessly managing everything from scheduling cleaning services to handling groceries and laundry and selecting the perfect décor to make our house feel like a home.

In return, I made it a point to show her how much I appreciated her. Every week, I would bring her fresh flowers, a small token to remind her of my gratitude and love. I would cook one of her favorite meals or experiment with a new recipe I had come across, hoping to surprise her with something special. It was my way of sharing a piece of my world with her, of balancing out the life we had built together.

Our evenings were our time to reconnect. After dinner, I would draw her a hot bubble bath scented with her favorite candles and accompanied by a glass of wine—a soothing nightcap to help her unwind after a long day.

It became a cherished ritual, a small act of love that signified the end of the day and the beginning of quiet moments just for us. Those evenings, filled with soft candlelight and the scent of lavender or vanilla, were a testament to how much she meant to me and how much we had created a life built on mutual respect, love, and appreciation.

In her absence, the weight of those responsibilities fell squarely on my shoulders, and I realized just how much she had managed so seamlessly. It wasn't just the household tasks I missed; it was how she brought warmth and comfort to our home. Every day was an adjustment as I navigated life without her steady presence, trying to honor the love we shared by keeping up with the little things she once cared for with such grace.

Becoming a widower brought a wave of challenges that affected every part of my life. Simple, routine tasks—things I once did without a second thought—suddenly felt overwhelming. My mind struggled to focus, and even the smallest responsibilities seemed monumental in the shadow of my grief.

On top of that emotional burden, there was also a financial adjustment I had to make. Losing my wife not only meant losing my partner but also the person who helped balance and support our household in countless ways. The weight of it all felt unbearable at times.

Though my mother and sister loved me deeply and did what they could to provide support, there was still a profound sense of loneliness that lingered. It wasn't that they didn't care; they just couldn't fill the unique void left by my wife. When you're fortunate enough to marry your best friend, someone who knows every part of you—your secrets, dreams, needs, and mood swings—it creates a bond that no one else can replace.

My wife understood me in a way that even family, with all their love and good intentions, couldn't. She had been my confidante, my rock, someone who saw me at my worst and celebrated me at my best.

Losing that kind of connection was devastating. Friends and family tried to comfort me, but the truth was, there's no substitute for a spouse who knows your soul inside and out. It's a level of companionship that's hard to explain to others, and their efforts, while appreciated, couldn't fill the emptiness I felt. Every day, I had to confront that absence—the person who once understood me better than anyone was no longer there, and it was a reality I wasn't sure how to navigate.

Time is said to heal all wounds, but in my experience, it felt as though time was dragging on painfully slowly. Each day seemed to blur into the next, and the weight of grief made it feel as though I was moving through quicksand. It took several months before I could even consider seeking professional help. Eventually, I reached out to a licensed therapist, recognizing that I couldn't navigate this journey of healing on my own.

In our sessions, she became a lifeline, offering me tools and insights that helped guide me through the darkness.

Grief is a deeply personal journey that can feel overwhelming, but by embracing certain principles, you can find your way through the pain toward healing.

1. Allow yourself to feel your emotions

Grief can bring an overwhelming flood of emotions, some of which may be intense or unfamiliar. It's essential not to suppress or avoid these feelings. Whether it's sadness, anger, or frustration, every emotion is valid in the grieving process.

It can be tempting to bury those feelings to move on quickly, but the only true path to healing is allowing yourself to feel them.

Grief isn't something you can outrun or ignore. By confronting these emotions head-on, you begin to process them, even though it may hurt deeply. This step is crucial because bottling up emotions often leads to more suffering in the long run, and avoiding them can stifle your healing process.

2. Don't be afraid to share your feelings and release them as they come

One of the greatest challenges after loss is the sense of isolation. You may feel as though no one truly understands what you're going through, or you might be hesitant to burden others with your pain. Speaking about your feelings is a necessary part of healing.

Sharing with trusted friends and family, or even through journaling, allows you to release the emotions weighing you down. You don't have to carry it all by yourself.

Whether through talking, journaling, or finding creative outlets to express your feelings, releasing those emotions helps prevent them from becoming an even heavier emotional burden. Sharing your grief can be incredibly liberating, reminding you that you don't have to go through this journey alone.

3. Focus on self-care: remove any negative people and anything toxic from your life

Grief can leave you emotionally and physically drained, and surrounding yourself with toxic influences or negative people only makes the healing process harder. Take time to reevaluate your environment and remove any negativity from your life. That may mean distancing yourself from people who are critical, unsupportive, or draining and letting go of habits or situations that contribute to your stress.

Self-care isn't just about pampering yourself; it's about protecting your peace of mind and creating space for healing.

Whether through meditation, exercise, or simply setting boundaries, focusing on self-care during grief is vital for restoring emotional balance. It also means creating a safe, positive space for yourself to heal at your own pace.

4. Stay busy with a hobby or discover a new one.

Grief can consume your every thought, making it feel as though you'll never escape its grasp. One way to combat this is by staying active, either with existing hobbies or by discovering new ones. Engaging in something enjoyable or learning something new provides a welcome distraction from the sadness. It gives a sense of purpose, even if only for a few hours.

5. Take your time—heal at your own pace

Above all, remember that healing is not a race. There's no set timeline for grief, no one-size-fits-all approach to moving forward.

It's easy to feel pressure from others or even from yourself to "get over it" or "move on," but that's not how grief works.

Allow yourself the space to heal at your own pace without comparing your journey to anyone else's. Avoid the trap of "Survivor's Remorse," where you might feel guilty for moving forward while your loved one is no longer here. Grieving is a deeply personal process, and there is no right or wrong way to do it. What matters most is giving yourself the grace to heal in your own time, however long that might take.

"Life After Death" is Jennifer's favorite album by The Notorious B.I.G., and for good reason. Released in 1997, just days after his untimely death, the double album showcases his incredible lyrical prowess and storytelling ability.

Chapter 9: Patience: "Tap In, Tune in and Turn On"

My journey into spirituality began at the age of 16, following a life-altering experience that shook me to my core. I was driving home from school on a narrow, two-lane road when an oncoming car, partially in my lane, forced me to jerk the steering wheel in a desperate attempt to avoid a collision.

The sudden movement caused my car to lose control on the slick, rain-covered road. It began spinning out of control, circling several times before crashing violently into a large oak tree on the passenger side at 70 miles per hour.

The force of the impact was so intense that the car wrapped around the tree, to the point where anyone who saw the wreck would have assumed no one could have survived. Against all odds, I not only survived but managed to climb out of the mangled wreckage, crawl up an embankment to the road, and flag down help.

Miraculously, I escaped with only a minor cut on my head and some bruising on my leg. Within two months, I was back at school and playing sports. When my mother first saw the remains of the car, her immediate thought was that I must have died in the crash—such was the extent of the damage.

The second incident occurred just a few years later when I once again found myself in close proximity to death. After leaving a nightclub, I was walking to my car when a gunfight erupted near me. The person walking beside me was shot and killed in an instant. Though the bullets could easily have struck me, I walked away unharmed.

Shortly after this, I was deployed to Iraq as part of one of the earliest U.S. ground forces to set foot there. My unit's mission was to scout locations, survey the terrain, and help build Forward Operating Bases (FOBs) for the military. This deployment marked the beginning of a new phase in my life, one filled with constant danger and the ever-present threat of death.

I witnessed numerous people lose their lives in combat, yet time after time, I was spared. Whether it was near misses from sniper fire, escaping the blast radius of IEDs, or avoiding random mortar attacks, I found myself repeatedly standing just outside the reach of death.

At times, it felt as though some unseen force was guiding my steps, ensuring that I survived while others did not. I experienced similar brushes with death during two subsequent deployments over the next ten years. In many situations, a shift in timing by mere seconds could have resulted in a much different fate.

It was during my second deployment that I began to seriously explore the deeper questions surrounding life, death, and the forces that seemed to be at play in my life. Encounters with different cultures, religions, and spiritual leaders, including shamans, sparked a desire within me to understand why I had been spared so many times when others had not. I immersed myself in books on ancient religious beliefs, universal powers, and spiritual teachings. This journey ignited a profound search for my true purpose. I began to question what role divine intervention or cosmic forces had played in my survival and what my life was meant to represent after so many close brushes with death.

These experiences set me on a path of spiritual reflection, one that has continued to evolve as I seek answers to the larger mysteries of life. Why was I spared? What does it mean to have survived so many life-threatening situations? And what is the purpose of the blessings and protection I have received? These questions continue to shape my journey as I search for meaning in my life and the unknown that lies ahead.

While reflecting on mental health and grief after an early morning teletherapy session, I came across an interesting fact: sunlight has a profound effect on mood and mental well-being by increasing serotonin levels in the brain. I learned that sunlight stimulates the retina, sending signals to the brain to produce serotonin, a neurotransmitter responsible for regulating mood, sleep, appetite, and digestion. What caught my attention was how serotonin plays the same role as the anxiety medication I had been prescribed for my mood.

However, I've never been one to rely on pills or pharmaceuticals. Even for something as minor as a headache, I've always preferred to seek out natural or herbal remedies.

So, instead of turning to medication, I embraced sunlight as part of my healing process. On sunny days, I would lay out my prayer mat in the backyard for my Zuhr prayer, the Muslim midday prayer. After completing my prayer, I would sit in the warmth of the sun, meditating for 15 to 30 minutes, allowing myself to absorb the sun's powerful energy. This practice became a key part of my routine, and I found that the sun's light felt almost mystical, lifting my spirits in ways I hadn't expected.

Another step I took in my healing journey was trying Reiki healing, a practice that taps into the body's energy forces to alleviate stress, reduce anxiety, and promote relaxation.

Reiki offered me a deeper sense of calm and balance, providing me with a natural way to manage emotional pain and stress without needing medication. These methods, along with my spiritual practices, became crucial to my overall mental and emotional well-being during that time.

In my mid-20s, I realized that I possessed empathic abilities, which shed light on the intense emotions I experienced during my adolescence. It also explained my natural ability to read and understand people's emotions on a deep level.

However, this gift wasn't without its challenges. Relationships were particularly difficult because I unknowingly absorbed all the emotional energy in the room, and without knowing how to channel or manage it, I often ended up sabotaging these connections. Over time, I found myself retreating into solitude, where I felt more at peace, free from the emotional energy of others.

It wasn't until my mid-30s, after gaining more wisdom about my empathic abilities, that I began to embrace and refine my gift. Rather than allowing it to disrupt my relationships, I started using my abilities to help others, pouring my energy into selfless acts instead of using my emotional insight to navigate personal relationships.

As I focused more on helping those I encountered, I noticed a deepening connection with God and the mystical forces of the Universe. This shift in mindset brought a series of blessings into my life, and moments of serendipity became a regular occurrence. It felt as though the Universe was rewarding me for my acts of kindness and my "pay it forward" approach to life.

Even when those I trusted betrayed me or acted in ways that lacked integrity, I consciously chose to let go without holding onto bitterness or resentment. Instead of dwelling on the hurt, I wished them well and moved on, knowing that carrying negativity would only block my own growth. My focus stayed on spreading positivity and using my empathic abilities to uplift others.

As I continued to live with this intention, I became more deeply attuned to the divine guidance around me and the subtle energy of the universe. This transformation reshaped how I approached relationships—choosing peace over conflict—and opened me up to a higher sense of purpose. I found myself aligned with a greater spiritual path, where my life became a vessel for healing, growth, and deeper connection with the forces that guide us all. This shift allowed me to fully enter my spiritual journey, leading to more meaningful experiences and a profound sense of alignment with the universe.

Over time, I developed specific techniques to help channel my emotions and quiet my mind, drawing heavily from African traditions and practices. These methods provided me with a sense of grounding and allowed me to manage my empathic abilities in a more balanced way. Here's a step-by-step description of some of the key practices I incorporated into my routine:

1. **Kinetic Yoga**: This practice, rooted in ancient African traditions, focuses on the connection between movement and breath. I would start by grounding myself, taking deep, slow breaths to center my mind, and then gradually moving into fluid, deliberate poses that encouraged my body to release pent-up energy. Kinetic Yoga helped me balance my emotions by aligning my physical and emotional state through mindful movement and breathwork. It became a powerful way to process the emotions I had absorbed throughout the day and release them without feeling overwhelmed.

2. **Massage and Bodywork**: I began incorporating bodywork into my healing process, specifically utilizing Ghanaian shea butter massages. The use of natural shea butter, rich in vitamins and deeply nourishing, added a healing element to the massages. The massage techniques

themselves focused on releasing tension stored in my muscles, helping to bring my body into a state of relaxation. This also allowed me to release accumulated emotional stress, as the body holds onto emotions just as much as the mind.

3. Buddhist Practices for Centering the Body

Borrowing from Buddhist traditions, I implemented focus breathing and body alignment exercises. These practices were essential for calming my mind and creating a sense of inner stillness. Focus breathing, in particular, helped me become more aware of my emotional state and shift my energy when I felt overwhelmed. I would sit in a quiet space, close my eyes, and concentrate on my breath—slowly inhaling through my nose, holding my breath, and then exhaling through my mouth. This simple act of mindful breathing helped me regain control over my emotions and reduce mental noise.

4. Chiropractic Sessions and Deep Tissue Massages

I incorporated regular chiropractic sessions and deep tissue massages to maintain a sense of physical and emotional balance. The chiropractic work helped with body alignment and reduced physical tension, while the deep tissue massages, including fascial release, worked to relieve deeper layers of tension that had built up over time. These sessions often left me feeling lighter, both physically and emotionally, as they released stored tension that I hadn't even realized I was carrying.

These practices became integral to my emotional and mental well-being, allowing me to channel the energy I was absorbing as an empath and quiet my mind, ultimately providing me a greater sense of peace and control over my gift.

My spiritual practices became a lifeline, helping me maintain focus and discipline during the darkest period of my life: grieving the passing of my wife. Although the pain I felt was deep, and I cried every day for months, I knew I had to keep moving forward. My motto became "Heal Forward," with the goal of "Healing while moving forward."

Life doesn't stop, even when you're in the midst of loss, and I realized I had no choice but to push ahead. The bills kept coming, and I found myself back in a single-income household, with financial pressures that didn't care about my grief. I couldn't afford to sink into a long depression; instead, I had to learn how to cope with my grief and transform this tragic experience into something life-changing.

Before my wife's passing, I had already been "tapped in and tuned in, courtesy of her," especially during the pandemic. While many were struggling, we were thriving as a couple.

By applying my spiritual teachings, I increased my net worth, purchased a larger home, and secured a promotion at work. It felt as though everything I touched during that time turned to gold because I was aligned with the universal powers.

After losing my wife, I remained committed to my spiritual journey, which helped me stay the course even amid grief. I didn't just survive—I grew. My mind became sharper, and I became a wiser, more reflective man.

I took up learning Italian, which challenged me to stay mentally engaged, and I deepened my meditation practice, reaching new levels of inner peace and mindfulness. At the same time, I let go of harmful habits that had once held me back, such as heavy drinking and poor eating habits, choosing instead to live a more balanced and health-conscious lifestyle.

Through all of this, I've become more fearless. I no longer walk this Earth with a fear of death. My faith and belief that if I stay "tapped in and tuned in," I'm protected by the same forces that have always guided me. The only thing I truly fear now is Allah. This transformation has helped me navigate my grief and set me on a path of continued growth, wisdom, and strength.

I no longer tiptoe through life or let negative people or thoughts dictate how I approach my day. In the past, I might have allowed others' negativity to impact my mood or decisions, but now I refuse to give that kind of control to anyone or anything. When things don't go my way or I face challenges, I don't get overwhelmed or sink into self-pity.

Instead, I remain calm, control my emotions, and think through solutions logically without dwelling on frustration or sorrow. Each situation becomes a learning experience rather than a reason to ask, "Why is this happening to me?"

I've come to realize that we're only in this physical form temporarily—this life is just the first stage of human evolution. With that understanding, I've shifted my focus toward the untapped potential of the human mind.

By accessing more of the mind's powers, I've learned to process events more clearly and easily. The more I explore these abilities, the more I can handle life's challenges with a calm and balanced mindset. I no longer let my emotions control how I react. I live by the "Duck on Water" analogy: while a duck seems calm on the surface, it's paddling furiously beneath the water.

Similarly, I may feel emotional turbulence inside, but outwardly, I remain composed, allowing me to think clearly and respond in a way that serves me best. This perspective has transformed the way I handle difficulties, helping me stay emotionally balanced and focused on the bigger picture.

Even though I've made great strides in my spiritual and personal growth, I'm still very much a typical human being. I wake up each day missing my "Twin Flame," my wife, and on certain days, especially Mondays, the weight of her absence feels heavier.

On those harder days, I allow myself to release the emotions and feelings that come with grief. Once I've gathered my composure, I move into my mental detox process—starting with morning prayer, meditation, workout, and finishing with deep breathing and stretching exercises to help reset my mind and body.

Although I lost someone who was a part of my world for over a decade, I've taken that tough life lesson and turned it into something positive, using it to help those around me. Her passing pushed me to achieve personal goals I may have never pursued because, before her death, I was living in a very comfortable space. I was blessed to have a wonderful life with her, and in a sense, I had entered a phase of semi-retirement.

We were planning our future together, looking forward to finding our dream home in a tropical location where we could disconnect from the everyday stressors of life.

Her passing changed everything, but it also ignited a deeper drive within me to live fully and use our shared life's lessons to influence and uplift others.

"Patience" by Damien Marley and Nas was one of our favorite songs together. We would have fun debates breaking down the lyrics and talking about what they meant to each of us. It was one of those special moments we shared, connecting over the deeper meanings of the song's message about time, understanding, and waiting for things to unfold. It always led to great conversations and brought us even closer.

Chapter 10: Life Goes On

Looking back on the past two years, I see a series of defining moments that transformed my path and perspective. Each pivotal experience reshaped me, fueling my growth and altering how I see the world, revealing just how far I've come and what has shaped me into who I am today.

Significant Moments in My Journey

- **Writing a Journal to Express and Release Emotions**: In the wake of my wife's passing, I turned to writing as a means of processing my grief. Keeping a journal became a way to express and release emotions that I had often kept hidden, including thoughts and memories I rarely shared with anyone else.

Through journaling, I allowed myself to confront complex feelings, from pain and sorrow to moments of peace and gratitude for the memories we created together. This practice not only helped me work through my grief but also became a deeply personal ritual, providing solace during the darkest days.

- **A Spiritual Ceremony at Boti Waterfalls in Ghana**: Seeking closure and a meaningful way to honor her memory, I traveled to Ghana to hold a private ceremony at Boti Waterfalls in the Yilo Krobo District. My wife was always intrigued by the Yoruba goddess Oshun, symbolizing love, beauty, fertility, and the life-giving force of water. Boti Falls, with its unique twin falls that represent both male and female energies, felt like the perfect place to release her remains. Local folklore holds that when these twin rivers meet, they create a rainbow—an embodiment of unity, harmony, and hope.

Placing her essence in a place so closely aligned with her spirit felt incredibly right, connecting her to a vital life source that nourishes the land and its people. Witnessing this union of nature gave me a profound sense of peace, as I knew her memory would live on as part of something essential and beautiful.

- **Embracing Cremation as a Spiritual Process**: My wife and I both viewed cremation as a deeply symbolic act, a liberation of the soul from its earthly confines. To us, it represented a return to nature and the divine—ashes to ashes, dust to dust. Completing this step allowed me to feel a sense of closure and acceptance in her passing. I no longer felt the weight of resentment or unresolved emotions, and for the first time, I could envision the possibility of a new beginning. On that day, as I let go of her physical form, I felt a profound shift in my heart, as if the next chapter of my life had quietly begun.

- **Rediscovering and Deepening My Islamic Faith**: One of the most grounding forces in my journey was my faith. My wife and I had explored Islamic teachings together, and after her passing, it was my connection to these teachings that provided me with the resilience and patience to cope with her loss. In Islam, I found guidance, fortitude, and an unwavering sense of purpose. It isn't a religion, as many outsiders may think; it's a way of life. If you're not willing to shed bad habits, how can you ever expect life-changing events to work in your favor? Remember, "Health is Wealth"—avoid falling into the trap of a "King's Disease" mindset.

My daily practices, prayers, and connection to the discipline of my faith became cornerstones of my healing. These spiritual practices reminded me of the impermanence of life and the continuity of the soul, and they offered me a new perspective on the "new normal" of my life. Rediscovering my faith and embracing its teachings fully enabled me to face each day with a renewed sense of strength and resolve.

Experiencing life-threatening events early on had a profound impact on me, instilling a deep sense of confidence and an unshakable mindset. Realizing I had no control over my "death date" freed me from the constant worry about dying. Instead, it fueled a sense of urgency about how I wanted to live, especially in my role as a father.

The hardest challenges of navigating my grief were overwhelming. Coming home to an empty house—a place once filled with love, joy, and peace—was now a reminder of loss, the very place where my wife had taken her last breath on the living room floor.

Adjusting to a new daily routine without someone to come home to, felt alien. Managing all the household duties and responsibilities alone and transitioning back to life as a single man came with its own set of struggles. Even the idea of opening myself to dating and romance again felt like an insurmountable hurdle.

In the midst of this journey, meditation, prayer, and empathy became essential lifelines, offering me a steady structure and a safe space to release the emotions I carried each day. Through these practices, I found a rhythm—a way to let go of the pain without letting it consume me entirely.

Meditation and spiritual reading provided a kind of sanctuary, helping me to process my grief and gradually organize my thoughts. They allowed me to sit with the raw intensity of my emotions, making them more bearable and less overwhelming.

Yet, alongside this practice of release, a heavy weight of guilt and survivor's remorse lingered, shadowing each step forward. I wrestled with an unspoken question: how long should I wait before allowing myself to move on? I feared that moving forward too quickly would somehow dishonor her memory as if my own healing would lessen the impact of her life on mine.

This internal conflict—this struggle between the need to heal and the desire to honor—proved to be one of the most challenging parts of my journey. Each day became a delicate balancing act as I learned to honor her memory while gradually, tenderly, learning to live again.

Emotionally, though I'm dating again with hopes of finding true love, I still carry scars and remain partially unavailable until I'm truly ready to open myself to love again. Finding the motivation to date without constantly comparing it to my past relationship was a challenge. Forgiving myself was key—I had to accept that I did everything I could to save her.

Dating has been complicated by my heightened empathy, which made my tolerance low and motivation even lower. I often found myself absorbing a mix of energies from each date—mostly negative—which left me needing a mental reset each time I got home.

Setting boundaries became essential, especially as I began to navigate the unfamiliar territory of dating as a widower. I made a conscious effort to be transparent about my mental and emotional state, understanding that anyone entering my life deserved honesty about where I was in my healing journey.

Instead of pursuing relationships with a sense of urgency, I adopted a more organic, even passive, approach, allowing connections to form naturally, without force or expectation. For me, it's unconditional or nothing. I came to realize that if I were to fall in love and marry again, it would have to be a relationship grounded in authenticity and a sense of ease—a love that feels both enduring and freely given.

I believe that genuine relationships aren't meant to be inherently difficult. While every relationship has its moments of challenge, the true struggles often arise when barriers such as poor communication or a lack of honesty enter the picture.

Open dialogue, transparency, and respect for each other's experiences lay the foundation for any lasting connection. Regardless of what we anticipate our partner's reaction might be, honest communication is crucial to building trust and understanding. It's in this space of mutual respect that a strong, resilient relationship can grow.

After my wife passed away, I felt a profound need to make changes that would support my overall well-being. I turned my focus inward, dedicating time and effort to improving my mental, emotional, and physical health. One of the most significant steps I took was to remove toxic influences from my life—people, environments, and habits that drained rather than uplifted me.

Creating this positive space allowed me to foster a sense of peace and resilience, enabling me to move forward even in the midst of my grief. It was a journey toward rebuilding from the inside out, establishing a healthier, more balanced life that would support me through both the struggles and joys to come.

Establishing a steady routine became essential, beginning with the five daily prayers of Islam—Fajr, Dhuhr, Asr, Maghrib, and Isha—which grounded me and brought consistency to each day. I also set aside time daily to meditate and spiritually cleanse, making sure to release any negativity before going to bed and addressing concerns as they arose.

Additionally, I refined my inner circle, keeping only those who brought genuine value and purpose into my life. I learned to love those who walked different paths from a respectful distance to include certain family members whose nostalgic memories once bonded us.

True happiness, I found, rests in the peace of mind and clarity that comes with knowing my new path and purpose. The discipline and wisdom I've gained over the years have redirected my journey for the better. Stepping out of my comfort zone to embrace new challenges, like writing and engaging more deeply with people, has brought a newfound sense of happiness and peace.

"Life is for living, not merely existing in it."

Her passing taught me that any moment could be our last, and with that realization, I made a commitment to no longer hold back due to comfort or fears of what might go wrong. Her death was a powerful reminder that life is fleeting and can be taken at any instant. It felt selfish to spend this precious time merely existing without true purpose or the drive to build a lasting legacy.

Now, I approach each day with renewed confidence, fearlessness, and purpose, honoring Jennifer's memory and carrying forward the lessons her life and death have taught me.

My actions are more intentional, and my words more direct. I speak my mind freely and without hesitation, guided by a sharper vision and a clear strategy. I know what I stand for and pursue it with conviction.

I live each day unafraid, embodying the mindset of a man with nothing to lose. This perspective, fueled by a deep sense of faith, empowers me to make decisions with courage and conviction. I approach each moment as if it were my last, fully aware of the fleeting nature of life, and I strive to live without regrets. This mindset has transformed how I engage with the world, allowing me to embrace opportunities and challenges alike with an open heart.

Now, everything I do is anchored in clear goals and consistent action. I've shed the weight of procrastination that once held me back, consciously pushing myself out of my comfort zone to confront new experiences head-on.

Each risk I take not only builds my confidence but also uplifts my spirit, contributing to my ongoing journey of “healing forward.” I’ve learned that discomfort can be a powerful catalyst for growth, and I welcome it as a necessary part of my evolution.

With each step I take, I strive to create a life driven by purpose and vision. I focus on what truly matters to me, setting intentions that align with my values and aspirations. This intentional living has instilled a sense of clarity in my actions, reminding me that every choice I make contributes to the broader narrative of my life.

I am determined to cultivate joy, forge meaningful connections, and pursue passions that ignite my spirit. In doing so, I aim to build a legacy that reflects not only my personal journey but also honors the love and lessons I’ve received along the way. Every day is an opportunity for renewal, a chance to shape a future that resonates with my deepest desires and aspirations, and I embrace it wholeheartedly.

In honoring Jennifer, I strive to be the man she was proud to call her husband and best friend. Her memory serves as both my inspiration and my guide, and I aim to embody the qualities that defined our relationship—respect, integrity, commitment, confidence, kindness, and honor. Each of these values is a cornerstone of the love we shared, and I am committed to building upon the solid foundation we established together.

Living this way allows me to keep her memory alive in a deeply meaningful manner. It's not just about remembrance; it's about actively integrating the principles we cherished into my daily life. By doing so, I cultivate a sense of purpose that resonates with her legacy. Every act of kindness I extend, every moment of integrity I uphold, and every commitment I fulfill serves as a tribute to the love and respect we shared.

As I move forward, I do so with strength and resolve, understanding that my journey is not just my own but also a continuation of ours. I reflect on the lessons she imparted—how to approach challenges with grace, how to treat others with empathy, and how to remain steadfast in the face of adversity.

In embracing these qualities, I honor not only Jennifer's memory but also the love that shaped me into who I am today. I carry her spirit with me, allowing it to influence my choices and actions, ensuring that her legacy continues to thrive.

Each step I take is infused with a sense of purpose that celebrates our journey together, propelling me forward as I navigate life with her memory as my guiding light.

"Life Goes On" by Tupac—our favorite hip-hop artist of all time—has always held special meaning for us. Tupac's lyrics capture the raw emotions of loss, resilience, and the journey of moving forward, themes that resonate deeply in our lives.

Made in the USA
Columbia, SC
22 April 2025

5b336644-e49a-462d-88ab-8bc00795ee58R01